The surprising new facts about pot that all teens and parents need to know.

It is estimated that 10 million people in the United States are regular users of marijuana. The use of pot is now so widespread that there are strong movements ready to pave the way for legal, machine-made marijuana cigarettes. Don Wilkerson, an experienced counselor of drug addicts, speaks to everyone regarding the solution for America's fastest-growing drug problem. Learn the latest reports about pot, and find out how you can deal with it effectively.

FACTS EVERY PARENT SHOULD KNOW ABOUT: marijuana

DON WILKERSON

Fleming H. Revell Company
Old Tappan, New Jersey

Unless otherwise identified, Scripture quotations in this volume are from the King James Version of the Bible.

Scripture quotations identified TLB are from The Living Bible, copyright © 1971 by Tyndale House Publishers, Wheaton, Illinois 60187. All rights reserved.

Scripture quotations identified NIV are from the HOLY BIBLE, New International Version, copyright © New York International Bible Society, 1978. Used by permission.

Excerpts from LISTEN magazine, © 1976, 1977, 1981 by Narcotics Education, Inc.

Material from *Focus on Alcohol and Drug Issues,* a publication of the U.S. Journal of Drug and Alcohol Dependence, Inc., Hollywood, Florida, is reprinted with permission.

Material taken from COUNSELING THE UNTAPPED GENERATION by David and Don Wilkerson (formerly published as "The Untapped Generation") Copyright © 1971 by Zondervan Publishing House. Used by permission.

Excerpts from *War on Drugs,* magazine of the National Anti-Drug Coalition, used by permission.

Quotations from *Toma Tells It Straight With Love,* $12.95, reprinted by permission of Books in Focus, 160 E. 38th Street, New York, NY 10016.

Excerpts from FAST TRACK TO NOWHERE by Don Wilkerson copyright © 1979 by Don Wilkerson, published by Fleming H. Revell Company.

Excerpts from MARIJUANA: THE SECOND TRIP, Revised Edition, © 1971 by Edward R. Bloomquist, M.D., reprinted with permission of Macmillan Publishing Co., Inc.

Excerpts from *Sensual Drugs,* by Hardin and Helen Jones, reprinted by permission of Cambridge University Press, © Cambridge University Press 1977.

Library of Congress Cataloging in Publication Data
Wilkerson, Don.
   Marijuana.

   Rev. ed. of: Shocking new facts about marijuana. 1980.
   1. Youth—United States—Drug use. 2. Marihuana.
3. Marihuana—Law and legislation—United States.
I. Title.
HV5824.Y68W54   1983   362.2′93   82–21627
ISBN 0–8007–5107–8

Copyright © 1980, 1983 by Don Wilkerson
Published by Fleming H. Revell Company
All rights reserved
Printed in the United States of America

Contents

1 One of the Most Dangerous Drugs   11

    Youth's Number-One Drug
    Updating the Figures
    Seven Effects of Pot Use
    Special Dangers of Marijuana
    Public Tolerance Toward Marijuana Use
    Needed: Knowledge and Action
    Failure of Education Programs
    Types of Tokers

2 Reefer Madness   28

    The Drug's Origins
    Federal Controls
    Rowell's Claims
    Varying State Laws
    Using "Reefer Madness" to Protect Pot
    The Drug Revolution and Public Indignation
    Change in Attitude Today
    Drugs in Sports
    Drugs in the Work Place
    Reasons for Attitude Change

3 The Colombian ... Cuban ... Californian Connections   42

    Colombia Still Tops
    Cuba's Connection
    High Profits Draw "Businessmen"
    The Crowded Airlanes

Also by Sea
Pot Farmers
Effectiveness of Enforcement
Pot's New Industry

4 Grass Roots   51

Effect of Decriminalization Laws
More Smokers Are Younger
Stronger Stuff
Pot and Teens
Burned Out
The Pot Life-Style
Pot and Crime
The New "High" Class?
Legalization—Then What?

5 The Medical Case Against Marijuana   65

Past Studies
New Evidence of Pot Dangers
The La Guardia Report
Inconclusive Studies
Arguments That Pot Is Harmless
Set the Record Straight
Effect on the Brain, Sex and the Reproductive
   Organs, Lungs
Principal Dangers of Pot

6 Decriminalization—Blessing or Curse?   82

Difference Between Decriminalization and Legalization
Laws in Various States
Effect of New Decriminalization Laws
The Effects on Our Society
The Hows and Whys of Drug Dependency
Effects of Marijuana on Drivers
Marijuana Lobbyists

Contents 7

7 Parent Power 98

    End of Permissive Society?
    CDU and "Responsible" Use
    Return of Parent Action
    Toughlove
    Bob Evans Takes Up the Challenge
    A Concerned Chicago Cop
    The Vanishing Head Shops

8 How to Guard Kids Against Drugs 106

    Home Prevention Remedies
        Communicate a Value System
        Defusing Rebellion
        Listen
        Importance of Self-Esteem
        Be Firm and Consistent
        Be a "Model" Parent
        Don't Try to Be Perfect
        Being "Together"
    Is Your Teenager Using Drugs?
        Know the Warning Signals
        Don't Overreact
        Don't Ignore It
        Be Knowledgeable About Drugs
        Mental "Detoxification"
        Join a Parent-Action Group
        Tell the Lawmakers

9 The Courage to Say *No!* 121

    Resisting Drugs
    How to Say *No*
        Respect Your Body
        Keep Your Eyes on the Goalposts
        Guard Relationships
        A Reason to Say *No*
        "No" Power

Marijuana

1
One of the Most Dangerous Drugs

YOUNG VIOLINIST AT METROPOLITAN
OPERA HOUSE MURDERED
TEENAGERS PAY TO HAVE FATHER KILLED
TWO TEENAGERS KILLED IN CAR ACCIDENT

These three tragedies headlined in newspaper stories had one thing in common. Marijuana was either directly or indirectly involved in the loss of four lives—a beautiful, aspiring musician, a father, and two senior high-school students.

The violinist was brutally murdered by a young worker at the Metropolitan Opera House. He raped her and tossed her down an elevator shaft. The lawyer's defense of the young man indicted for the murder—who had never been in trouble before and whose arrest shocked the middle-class neighborhood where he lived with his parents—was based on the contention that he was high under the influence of marijuana and beer at the time and didn't know what he was doing.

Two teenagers, a brother and sister, in Cleveland, Ohio, paid another youth $60 to kill their father. The forty-one-year-old man was shot in the head with a .38 caliber handgun. According to the police, the two children then proceeded to go through their dad's pockets, took his $230 paycheck plus some $60 in cash and went on a ten-day spending spree, acquiring (among other things) a television set and various games.

When the fourteen-year-old girl and seventeen-year-old boy were asked why they did it, they answered, "Because he wouldn't let us do anything we wanted to do, like smoke pot."

A carload of teenagers going home from a school dance was

being driven by a seventeen-year-old known "pothead." While trying to negotiate a curve on the road, he lost control of the late model sports car, crashed into a tree, killing himself and one other occupant.

Youth's Number-One Drug

Marijuana—pot—tea—hash—reefer—grass is the number-one drug of choice among American youth. Killing for it, as in the above stories, is an extreme and bizarre result of marijuana smoking but nevertheless, millions of youth and an increasing number of adults are endangering their lungs, brains, reproductive organs, and their lives (and those of others) by the habitual abuse of smoking brown grass rolled into a homemade-type cigarette.

Over the last decade marijuana use and abuse has risen to a frightening level. In 1977 the National Institute of Drug Abuse (known as NIDA) reported that 28 percent of youngsters between the ages of 12 and 17 have used marijuana. Four percent of the survey of 12- to 13-year-olds smoked it "during the past month." And one in nine high-school seniors smoked daily. Teenage marijuana use had doubled since 1965. However, since that report, marijuana use has sharply risen again. In some schools it's hard to find one in nine who do not smoke pot, at least occasionally. A friend who works on a college campus told me, "I am now so used to pot smoking, I guess I just take it for granted. It's the norm there."

According to a New York State survey conducted by the State Division of Substance Abuse, two out of three college students have used illegal drugs of one type or another. The survey of the college student drug usage indicated that marijuana (59 percent), hashish (28 percent), stimulants such as prescription amphetamines (21 percent), and cocaine (20 percent) were the drugs most frequently used in the six months preceding the study. The results further indicated that cocaine, prescription amphetamines, and marijuana attracted the largest number of new users.

Marijuana is now also becoming the norm in high schools. In report after report from students in high schools, I am told, 80 to 90 percent of the kids smoke marijuana. It is not uncommon to find eight- and nine-year olds smoking pot as well. The schools are permeated with it and it's filtering down to the elementary level. David

Toma, one of the outstanding drug-education speakers in the schools writing in *Toma Tells It Straight—With Love,* states:

> You parents, if you have children of school age, the odds are overwhelming that they are experimenting with drugs now or soon will be. The numbers are astronomical. Eighty-five percent of kids over 10 years old experiment with drugs. By the time a child's in the seventh grade, the odds are 50–50 that he's gone beyond the experimental stage and is now a regular user. If you think it's impossible that your child is in the wrong side of that statistic, then you're living with your head in the sand.

In a 1977 study on marijuana use entitled *The Seventh Annual Report on Marijuana and Health,* it found *43 million Americans had tried marijuana at least once and about 16 million had used it within one month of the survey.* Comparing this with previous findings, marijuana use among teenagers was reported to have increased by one-third and the report estimated that there were *ten million regular users.*

Updating the Figures

But these figures are now outdated! Recent estimates indicate an increase of marijuana use *another* one-third. No one knows for sure, but millions now smoke pot either casually, chronically, or crazily.

The above report on marijuana said a composite portrait of the most frequent pot smokers shows a college-educated white male, age twenty-two to twenty-five living in the west. However, *now* there is no composite portrait of a pot smoker. They range from the typical street youth to secretaries, factory workers, housewives, businessmen, middle-aged white- and blue-collar workers, and especially students. More recent surveys estimate that 68 percent of those in the age thirteen-to-twenty-five bracket have puffed marijuana at one time or another.

From all available evidence, we now know what drug educators and counselors have been warning—marijuana is so widespread, it has become the new alcohol of this era. Not that it is replacing alcohol, for youthful consumption of alcohol has risen. But it has taken the place of cigarettes among youthful puffers and inhalers. Some adults refer to regular cigarettes now as "sissy cigarettes," meaning they are into smoking pot. Therefore, parents get ready! Marijuana, machine-packaged by a leading tobacco company, may soon be on its way to your neighborhood store with the United States Seal of Approval stamped right on it. The move has been on by a well-funded lobby to have Congress pass a new federal marijuana decriminalization law. This is intended to lead eventually to a total legalization of the drug.

Will they succeed?
Can we stem the tide of drug abuse?

If we don't stop marijuana's widespread use and the tolerant attitude of society towards it, including the possibility of decriminalization or legalization, what will this mean to our society? What will it mean to our children? How will it affect future generations?

Seven Effects of Pot Use

What have been the short-term and long-term effects of its use? These and other questions must be faced *now*. More and more parents are refusing to sit back and allow their children to "go to pot." As the results of marijuana's widespread use and abuse unfold (while police, school authorities, law-enforcement agencies, community leaders, and parents have sat back and allowed it to happen), the minds and bodies of millions of abusers have borne testimony to its dangers and eventual devastation. The jury determining marijuana's case has been out for the last ten years or so, and now it's time to examine the hard evidence and come in with a verdict. Dr. Robert L. DuPont, former director of NIDA, stated:

> While Americans are debating the questions of criminal penalties for marijuana possession, the real tragedy has overtaken us almost unnoticed.... The real danger is the health danger posed by the epidemic danger of at least two kinds. One is the effects of the intoxication, ranging from the hazardous impact on driving to caring less about everything. The other area is purely physical. Here the concerns range from the regular oc-

currence of chronic bronchitis among marijuana smokers to the very real possibility of harmful effects ... and possible cancer.

Smoking one marijuana joint is equivalent to smoking one pack of cigarettes. *Five joints (of marijuana) have the same effect as smoking 112 tobacco cigarettes.*

The danger of marijuana's physical effect on the abuser is not the only evidence that demands a verdict. Here is a list of some effects marijuana use and abuse is having in our society:

1. **Student school dropout.** Marijuana turns the mind, will, and motivation to "mush." That is, regular users just don't care about anything anymore. They enter into a never-never land of neutrality to all reality.

2. **Absenteeism and impaired job performance.** More and more pot smokers are working-class youth and adults. They are trying to build automobiles, work on machines, or type letters while under the drug's influence. Others hold important and strategic positions in hospitals or, for example, a nuclear plant. Business and industry is just now waking up to this fact and trying to deal with the growing loss of time and job performance due to drug abuse.

3. **Injury and physical deterioration of talented athletes.** On both the amateur and professional level, the prevalence of drug abuse in almost all of the major sports is common knowledge. Such drugs as marijuana and cocaine are having an adverse effect on the ability of athletes to perform their skills.

4. **Cancer, and other damages to the lung, brain, and other parts of the body.** (See chapter 5, "The Medical Case Against Marijuana.")

5. **Sexual burnout.** There is shocking new evidence of the effect of the long-term use of marijuana on the male sperm and with females, on the unborn child.

6. **The economic cost.** The sale of marijuana, which is all part of what is called the "underground economy," has created an illegal industry that is estimated to outrank many of the legitimate indus-

tries in our country. (The profits from marijuana's sale, of course, are all tax free.)

7. The danger to America's military defense. Our nation's defenses have been and are impaired by the use and abuse of drugs in all branches of the military services. Airplanes, ships, weapons, and other equipment are being operated and maintained by military personnel who are abusers of marijuana and other drugs.

For these reasons (which will be explored in more depth) and others, there is no doubt in my mind that marijuana today is *one* of the *most* dangerous drugs that is being used by young and old alike.

- It is not the quick killer as is heroin.
- It does not damage the brain as fast as pills.
- It does not addict as does cocaine and other so-called hard drugs.
- It does not have the dangerous reputation as do some other drugs such as LSD or angel dust.

Special Dangers of Marijuana

Why then is it so dangerous? Simply because, when compared to other hard drugs, it is not as dangerous. Comparing drug with drug, marijuana is mild, for example, in comparison to heroin, barbiturates, LSD, PCP, or Quaaludes—that is like comparing degrees of dynamite or gun powder, however.

Marijuana's danger is in the subtle, uninformed way that its users indulge in it. It is so abused because it is low on the danger list of drugs. This lackadaisical attitude towards marijuana has led to a climate of tolerance to its possible dangers by those who smoke it and a society that condones it. In some circles, it is smoked as freely and openly as cigarettes. The pushers don't have to hang out in the shadows of the school yard to sell their wares. They can do it in the school bathroom, gym, or even the teachers' lounge. The secretary or clerk on Wall Street does not have to go to Harlem to connect. Pot, pills, and especially cocaine are available with ease right in the middle of the financial district. Students in small towns or rural

One of the Most Dangerous Drugs

areas don't have to go off to the big city to buy their ounce or whatever of pot. Business is booming locally.

According to a study done in 1980 by NIDA, illicit drugs are increasing rapidly in rural areas and may soon equal the similar kinds of problems usually associated with metropolitan areas.

Literally, our youth may be "going up [or down] in smoke." In addition to the rise of the use of marijuana over the last decade, the use of cocaine, pills, alcohol and especially angel dust is on the increase. An estimated 30 to 40 percent of American teenagers abuse alcoholic beverages. Approximately one-half million may be alcoholics. Thus, we have a drug combo—pot, booze, pills, angel dust, and other dangerous narcotics taking its toll on our children. *The loss of youthful minds, bodies, and souls through the use of drugs is one of the worst tragedies in modern history.* And it is happening without most parents really knowing its full impact on our youth and our society.

Public Tolerance Toward Marijuana Use

Can this epidemic be stopped? Will decriminalization of marijuana inevitably lead to legalization? Yes, it will!—*unless* the moral trends that have prevailed in our nation over the last two decades begin to change. Because of the lessening of the penalties associated with the use and sale of marijuana in recent years, it has been and gets easier and easier to obtain. Marijuana is probably the largest industry of at least one South American country (the source of the majority of the grass presently being smuggled into this country). Several U.S. agents were killed in that country while they were trying to work with the government on the curtailing of the drug trade. In a more recent development, marijuana has become the new illegal U.S. farm crop that's booming. Therefore, with or without legalization, marijuana is plentiful.

Community and school authorities have winked at the abuse of marijuana on college campuses and in high schools. Most act as if they don't know or want to know what is going on. (One school that had the courage to search for marijuana by sending in trained dogs to sniff for it was hit with a lawsuit by civil libertarians for invasion of privacy.)

This public tolerance has had law enforcement people confused.

In April 1979, the city of Berkeley, California, passed legislation requiring the police to make enforcement of state marijuana laws there "lowest priority." The law passed by a substantial margin.

Without the moral support and the backing of the community at large, the police lack the necessary incentive to carry out whatever form of law does exist to keep drugs away from our youth and keep our schools and youth hangouts from being an open marketplace for the sale and distribution of not just pot but other dangerous narcotics.

In general, there has been for the past decade a tolerance towards the use of marijuana in particular and drugs in general. Never before has society so changed its mind and attitude about a dangerous (or, at least, a potentially dangerous) drug such as marijuana. We have gone from a *tough* stand against it in the sixties to a *tolerance* of it in the seventies and the prospects of its *legalization* in the eighties! (I'll explain a few of the reasons for this turnabout later.)

Have we made a mistake about our tolerance towards marijuana? The evidence is that we have. Walter X. Lehmann, M.D., states in a 1979 *Reader's Digest* article entitled "Marijuana Update":

> Anyone who says "pot" is harmless would get an argument from me. It hasn't been harmless to any of the 3,000 young people I've worked with as a specialist in adolescent medicine. Virtually all who become addicted to hard drugs started with marijuana, which distorted their judgment and put them into the drug scene. But I've learned that marijuana by itself is bad enough—its effect too often subtle and insidious, with long-range damage difficult to calculate.

Teenager—if you're smoking marijuana, you owe it to yourself to read these shocking new (and some old) facts about pot. There are some things your friends who use and introduce you to it never would tell you about its effects. Don't be stubborn and have to learn the hard way, as many unfortunately do. Before you get deeper and deeper into the drug scene, take the time to read what some "experts" are saying about marijuana. By *experts,* I'm not just talking about doctors, researchers, or drug educators. I'm also referring to present and past pot smokers who are living testimonies of what marijuana did to them.

If you're a nonsmoker but being pressured day after day in school to "toke," then I urge you to know the truth and nothing but the truth about pot. There is no rainbow ahead of this kind of gold. The first-time or new users see only the "high" or happy side of marijuana's effect. Long gone from the pot parties are the past users. Many have "graduated" and gone on to bigger and worse things. They are no longer members of the "high" society. They have joined the "low" society. But your friends and the pushers will not tell you about *them*.

Parents—it's time too for you to wake up! Face the facts that are right before your eyes. *Marijuana is one of the most dangerous drugs.* We know this because the kids themselves—the abusers—are walking around as human labs or evidence of its dangers. David Toma says:

> While psychologists and social scientists try to create "theories" to explain the reasons for the drug use, the physical scientists will spend the next 30 years looking into their microscopes and fiddling with their rhesus monkeys to make sure that they don't "prematurely" condemn any of the drugs the kids are using.
>
> In the meantime, the epidemic grows. In the meantime, the kids are dying! They can't learn or grow up! In the meantime, more kids become mental, emotional and physical cripples!
>
> We don't have to wait three decades to condemn marijuana. We don't have to wait for the monkeys and lab rats to tell us that grass screws up their heads!
>
> The kids are telling us right now! The kids are telling us everything we have to know and we are out of *our* minds if we don't listen to them!

Needed: Knowledge and Action

Since we have not been able to depend on the government to protect our children from marijuana (either by stepped-up detention of the smuggling trade or enforcement of the laws), as concerned parents we must prepare a moral and spiritual defense against it.

The first step is to *get the facts!* It is important to become as knowledgeable about its dangers as possible, yet at the same time not panic or overreact if and when a teenager is found to be trying it. Given the choice between overreaction and inaction, I would rather see the former. But it does not have to be either. Parents all across the country are waking up and getting involved in trying to get the facts about drugs. (See chapter 7, "Parent Power.")

The next step is to *do something!* Parents must do something *before* drugs break out and, of course, must know what to do when the child is already experimenting or is a regular user.

In an editorial statement of the magazine *Focus on Alcohol and Drug Issues* (January–February 1982) the publisher says:

> The recent parent-power revolution taking place in this country is all too clearly demonstrating the cogent force parents, neighborhoods and communities can bring to bear on adolescent drug abuse. And, the influence of the parents' group movement is being felt all the way from the local community to the halls of the Capitol. Historically, prevention-education specialists have voiced the critical need for parent involvement and commitment—It's now here and it's growing rapidly.

There are nearly a thousand different parent groups nationwide that have banded together to fight back against drug abuse. Their impact is being felt. This is an encouraging sign.

Most of all, we have to teach our youth *before the fact rather than just react after the act.* Our youth need inner mechanisms and inner controls against the temptation to experiment with marijuana (since this is usually the lead-in to other more potent drugs) and other artificial "highs" in general (such as booze). In the final analysis, it is the inner legislation of the heart that acts as a policeman or deterrent to help us and our kids to keep away from forbidden fruit. When there is no market for drugs, the supply dries up.

We need a moral and spiritual "renewal" to hit our schools, communities, and churches. Kids need to see that "straight" is the only life-style that guarantees a future survival. We need to pray for,

One of the Most Dangerous Drugs

work for, and support a new generation of kids who are made aware of what drugs have done to their older brothers and sisters and to a past generation—and begin a campaign for abstinence. The best way to fight fire is with fire. Kids take drugs because of its availability and the peer pressure resulting from its widespread use. One of the most effective deterrents is counter peer pressure. If even a small group of kids or students in a school make a pledge to "keep off the grass," it can have a remarkable effect on other kids. If the market is wiped out, drugs will be wiped out. This is getting to the source at the other end. There is little hope of cutting off the supply of marijuana where it's grown, but it can be cut off at the other end—where it normally is smoked. No sales—no smoke!

What if prevention fails? What if our children refuse to accept preventative measures or the Christian-Judeo standards that teach, preach, and practice against it. Worse, what if parents discover the teenager has gone beyond experimentation and has become a chronic user or is even taking other hard drugs?

It takes a very mature parent to face the trauma of drug addiction in the home. There are no easy answers or easy steps to solve the problem. Some children get worse before the situation can ever get better. The parents are often helpless, when their son or daughter runs away, gets immersed in the drug scene, or ends up in a hospital or jail.

This does not mean something cannot and should not be done. No matter what, parents must always try to "do something." They must always be ready and willing to help when the addict wants that help. It is Mom's and Dad's reaction to drug abuse and drug addiction in the home that is often the key to helping the youth if and when he or she is ready for that help.

When it comes to marijuana, the parent can begin by acquiring as much knowledge about the drug as possible. Neither ignorance nor emotional overreaction to a child's pot smoking will help matters. We must face the reality of raising kids in the eighties. Drugs, especially marijuana, are probably here to stay. All kids—Christian or non-Christian—churchgoing or nonchurchgoing—have to face the drug issue.

Therefore, all parents must work out a strategy to protect their kids. Drug abuse today often has little to do with the failure of parents to raise their kids properly. It has more to do with the failure of society to deal with drug abuse. It is a symptom of our times. The best of homes and the best of parents can raise a child with the highest of standards, meeting the child's emotional and spiritual needs, only to see the grown youth get involved in the abuse of drugs when at school or away at college.

While we must deal with the results of those who have already abused drugs, efforts must be concentrated on the upcoming generation.

Failure of Education Programs

This is the purpose of this book. We have tragically assumed that drug-education and prevention programs do not work. Since the first outbreak of drugs among the middle-class in the sixties, there has been a flood of materials, programs, and proposals to solve the problem. Before this (and when the problem was confined primarily to the inner city and the ghettos), it was virtually ignored. When the drug-abuse circle widened, we were unprepared for it. Many parents refused to believe when it began happening in lily-white America. When the full impact of drug abuse was finally recognized, crash programs of all sorts were instituted. Schools began drug-education classes. Community prevention programs were launched, as well as rehabilitation programs established.

What good such programs did or what effect these programs and materials had on prevention to stop further drug abuse is suspect. They probably had few positive results, primarily because the programs came too late. Some people say they had no effect at all. The fear then was that drug-education programs might make kids even more curious about drugs and thus they would go out and try them as a result. Most drug-education programs were one-shot deals containing misinformation and scare tactics that turned most kids off.

If the publishing of drug materials, lectures, films, rap sessions, and the presentation of drug-education programs did anything, they made us aware that there *was* a problem. And there still is. But now, with the public tolerance towards drugs, plus funding cutbacks for school and community drug-education programs, we have not been able to keep current on the data on hand that should be taught to students in the schools and made available to parents and families. Drug abuse, with marijuana leading the way, seems to have become another vice and abuse added to our social ills that is here to stay. Like crime, pornography, prostitution, and homosexuality—marijuana has been added to the acceptable moral ways of society that too many feel we're just going to have to "live with."

Since public attention has been turned aside from drugs, due to our preoccupation with rising inflation, the energy crisis, the nuclear debate, and other national and international problems—it is time once again to take a closer look at American youth and see what they are up to. The "baby boom" may be over but still one thing is for sure—kids are still going "up in smoke." It is time to wake up. The promarijuana advocates have made great headway, changing the attitude of Americans and legislators towards marijuana. The campaign to decriminalize pot has had the result that most states changed outdated (and much-needed revision) of old marijuana use and possession laws. But the result of these changes has given us much more than was bargained for. We have, in effect, given tacit consent to the promiscuous use of marijuana.

Therefore I say: **Americans—wake up!**
Parents—wake up!
School officials—wake up!
Community leaders—wake up!
Kids—wake up!

We are being inundated by a drug revolution. Drugs are killers! Ask Elvis's family! Ask John Belushi's wife and family! James Arness's daughter took too many pills and never woke up again. Liquor and drugs killed Diana Barrymore, and Art Linkletter's daughter jumped to her death doing an LSD trip. Most have heard and read about Carol Burnett's daughter's bout with drug addiction as well as the sad case of "One Day at a Time" star Mackenzie Phillips's struggle with narcotics. The best and the brightest of our stars have not been able to handle drugs—neither can our kids.

We are a nation of boozers—that is bad enough. Now we have added another crippling vice to society's ills. Enough is enough!

We may not be able to stop the moral landslide of drug abuse completely—probably far from it. But we can at least let our kids know our opposition to it. In the process, it is possible to save the minds and lives of thousands of our youth and our younger children who will inevitably follow the path we set for them. I can't change the alcoholic laws in our country, but I can preach and promote a moral philosophy against its use and abuse which will list voluntary abstinence. We must do no less in respect to the use and abuse of marijuana.

This does not mean we should give up trying to prevent its legalization or that we cannot pressure our schools and legislators to enforce the present laws against its abuse. We can! We all know that governmental bodies respond to the pressure groups in our society. I admire what one community in Indiana had the courage to do. As I mentioned earlier, the police, in cooperation with the high-school authorities, conducted a room-by-room search for drugs, using trained German shepherds and Doberman pinschers in the surprise raid. A controversy followed the action when the American Civil Liberties Union threatened to bring a lawsuit against the police and school officials. They claimed the rights of 2,780 students were violated.

A group of parents then rose up in support of the school administration. "The schools have been pussyfooting for years and not doing anything about the drug problem, and I fully support the raids," said one father who had a child in the school. "I have no concern about the students' rights being violated," he said. "Why should my kids have to be exposed to drugs?"

Another mother, with one child in the junior high school and another in the elementary school, commented: "If the ACLU wins, drugs will flow like water in Indiana. Fear, tempered with respect, like the fear of God will help the children avoid a tragedy like drugs."

Hats off to that town and those parents! Others apparently are following this tougher course. Parent-pressure groups have succeeded in getting a number of states to pass antidrug-paraphernalia laws to shut down stores that deal in drug paraphernalia associated with marijuana smoking and other abused drugs.

Many parent groups and neighborhood action groups need to serve notice to federal, state and local governments that they are not going to tolerate drug abuse. When they do, we will begin to see a reversal of present trends which have created a generation of pot smokers.

Unless and until the federal and state governments are willing to resist the decriminalization-legalization campaign-pressure groups and local communities let school authorities know they want drug abuse curbed, more and more of our kids will be challenged to toke a joint.

To better understand how far and how much marijuana is being used and abused among today's youth, here is a breakdown on the current pot scene. Here four different types of marijuana smokers are categorized.

Types of Tokers

The willing abuser. This is not the innocent peer-pressured kid who doesn't know what he is getting into. This is the kid that looks for escape through whatever is at hand. He usually starts in early adolescence and moves on fast and furious into the total drug scene. Usually this young person is searching for anything to get high and/or escape from life. This is the mixed up, lonely, emotionally starved youth, often the victim of a poor home environment. Rebellion and bitterness may also motivate the abuse of drugs. He (or she) uses marijuana and often other drugs to act out and "get even" with parents or society for the bad deal he feels he has been dealt.

Pot smoking in this case is only the symptom of a much deeper need and problem. Peter is just an example. His father was a drug addict. One day he and his brother discovered his father's nude body lying on the bathroom floor with a needle protruding from his arm. He had taken an overdose. While his father survived that incident, Peter did not. At the age of thirteen, he began smoking marijuana. "I smoked for four years," he said. "I would smoke whatever I could get my hands on. This eventually led to my robbing to get money for the smokes. This got me in and out of jail."

Among such abusers is the "don't confuse me with the facts; my mind is already made up." No matter how many times they are warned or what harm they see drugs doing to others, they have a *need* to get high. In fact, for some, the more dangerous, bizarre, or risky the drug trip, the more they will respond. As one young man put it, "Drugs did not look for me, I looked for them."

The abuser needs special attention and counsel and perhaps a Christian rehabilitation program. Many have to hit rock bottom or get worse before they can get better and will admit they need help and submit to those who can help.

The willing abuser of marijuana represents 25 to 30 percent of youth between the ages of thirteen and thirty-five.

The user. Millions now smoke pot in the same manner and for the same reasons people drink—for its pleasure and a temporary high. These are often referred to as the "recreational" users. Just as many teens and adults view sex as a mere pleasure to be indulged in at will (called recreational sex), so it follows that pot is smoked with the same promiscuous motivation and attitude. These include the "weekender," the "party smoker," and the "event smoker" (such as those who attend rock concerts or sporting events as an excuse to enjoy pot). Marijuana is more and more replacing tobacco as a smoker's weed of choice.

This occasional user is usually a young adult student or blue- or white-collar worker.

Dr. Edward R. Bloomquist, in his excellent book *Marijuana: The Second Trip,* identifies three types of users:

> Antisocial misfits, the "lower-caste" group (i.e. uneducated and usually unemployed and poorly motivated), who have from the beginning used the drug as an added chorus to the already established refrain of antiauthoritarianism, antidisciplinarianism, and antisocial activities.
>
> The "upper caste" ... who is far more interested in the use of the drug for self-exploration, mind expansion, and sociorelaxation.... In addition to committed users, we find the intellectuals, pseudointellectuals, and religious and pseudoreligious people. This group tends to pursue a search for inner truth and inner peace.
>
> The third group is the largest. It is composed primarily of average, curious, uninhibited people out for a lark. These youngsters are usually "chippers," that is, they play with the drug now and then as the mood directs them.

According to the latest NIDA figures, 68 percent of those in the thirteen to twenty-five age bracket have puffed marijuana at one time or another. Of the total number of marijuana smokers, my own personal estimate is that approximately 40 percent fall into the category of a *user*.

The "straight" kid. This is the young person who does not use drugs because he or she has no need or desire for it. This is the committed youngster. The commitment may be to God, to church, to acquiring an education, to sports, to a boyfriend or a girl friend, to marriage, or any other worthwhile goal. This is the child that is often motivated by spiritual and moral principles and whose needs are thus being met by the legitimate and natural (or supernatural) blessings of life. This young person usually does not have to worry about the temptation to use drugs, because he or she is so stimulated and turned on by such a commitment to follow the straight and narrow way.

Unfortunately, this type of young person is increasingly in the minority. The peer pressure to indulge in drugs is often so strong in some places that it takes almost a "supersaint" to withstand such pressures. The percentages of youth in this category range from a low 5 percent to a high of 30 percent, depending upon the school or community.

The undecided. In the late seventies, this category of the undecided or "in-betweener" represented the largest group of youth. By the early eighties this had changed. Those who once were uncertain as to the use and experimentation of marijuana joined the ranks of user and abuser. Whereas the undecided represented 50 to 60 percent of our youth, now they represent only 20 to 25 percent.

The undecided are those who have to fight tremendous pressure and the philosophy that "everybody's doing it." As with any youth fad or practice, not to go along with the crowd is to be made to feel guilty. The undecided youth feels caught between the need to be popular and accepted by peers and the responsibility to obey parents and/or God. *This* is the youngster who should be the primary focus of attention. He or she is up for grabs. He is the reason schools, churches, parents, and community organizations must develop counter-peer-pressure groups to help the morally and spiritually weakening youth resist the seductive pressure of friends and classmates.

This also *may* be the youngster who has all the outward appearances of being okay but is quietly and secretly smoking a joint at a party, dance, or being turned on by a friend. Most users and abusers are not introduced to drugs (especially marijuana) by some sleazy-looking street pusher, but by a known and even trusted friend.

The undecided youth who does give in to the users can be reached if something is done soon enough, especially before the initial guilt wears off and the youth culture makes him feel his habit is no big deal.

Usually by the time a student reaches junior high school, the decision has to be made regarding use or nonuse of marijuana. Therefore, the largest category of undecided are those coming out of elementary school.

It is to the user and the undecided that this material is being prepared for use by parents, counselors, and all who are concerned about the pressure our children and youth are under in schools and in their communities. To smoke or not to smoke is one of those pressures. I hope both adult and teenager will take good advice in the pages that follow. Proverbs 10:8 (Good News Bible) says, "Sensible people accept good advice...." Given the right information, our youth are capable to make the right decisions regarding pot smoking.

And given the right spiritual perspective on life, they can become sensible people, ready to accept good advice. I agree 100 percent with the statement: "Fear, tempered with respect, like the fear of God, will help the children avoid tragedy like drugs."

2
Reefer Madness

Some may wonder why all the whoopla about pot. Why the controversy surrounding it? What has caused the emotionally charged debate around this strange weed? What is "reefer madness"?

In 1935, a low-budget film called *Reefer Madness* portrayed the so-called evils of marijuana. It declared that pot smoking led to murder, rape, suicide, and other similar evils. Today the movie has become a pot-culture feature shown in thousands of college theaters and movie houses—as well as at pot parties—as a parody of the falsehoods and paranoia that once surrounded the use of marijuana.

Why the paranoia? Where did it originate?

The Drug's Origins

A brief history of *Cannabis sativa* (Latin for "canelike" and "cultivated"), the hemp plant from which the marijuana weed is produced, provides some insight on how reefer madness originated. The earliest writings referring to *Cannabis sativa* date as far back as 2700–2500 B.C. According to Paul Dennis and Carolyn Berry in *The Marijuana Catalog,* "Credit for the first use of marijuana should probably go to the nomadic people of the Central Asian plains, who spread the weed through China and later to India. By 2500 B.C., Indian culture was full of religious songs and hymns praising the use of *soma,* which by all indications was *Cannabis.*"

Marijuana's entrance into the Western culture was in the 1900s, when the plant was widely grown in Virginia, presumably for its fiber, which was used to make rope. It is reported that George Washington grew it as a cash crop because of its fiber use. *The Marijuana Catalog* states: "It was no more regarded as a plant drug than the Morning Glory."

Also in the mid-1800s the plant appeared in a new form, as a medicine for a wide variety of ailments, and was listed in drug-reference manuals of that time. The extract of hemp was reportedly used in treating such ailments as gout, rheumatism, epidemic cholera, and other ailments. In Poland, Russia, and Lithuania, hemp was used to treat toothaches by inhaling the vapor from seeds thrown into hot stones. Larry Sloman observes in *Reefer Madness:*

> In New York City during the 1920s, it was not uncommon for Russian and Polish immigrants to trek over to Nassau Street, buy bulk Cannabis, return to their Lower East Side tenements, throw the Cannabis on the radiator, using a towel to form a smoke chamber and inhale the fumes for respiratory ailments.

As a medicinal agent, marijuana generally fell into disfavor before the turn of the century. For one, it was insoluble and therefore could not be injected, so there were delays of three hours when administered orally. Secondly, there was tremendous difficulty in standardizing the dosage, as different batches showed variations in potency. Also, there were variations among individuals in their response to the drug. So, when the new synthetic drugs were introduced—drugs which like morphine, were capable of administration by the newly discovered hypodermic syringe—Cannabis use decreased.

However, as a recreational drug, Cannabis was just beginning to be discovered by adventurous Americans.

In the twenties, jazz vocalists were singing about the elusive "reefer man," and by the thirties, marijuana continued to be popular among jazz musicians and immigrants from Jamaica and the West Indies, where it was quite prevalent and where they learned to acquire a taste for it. For them, it was a part of their life-style, but in America, they stayed outside the mainstream of society and so did marijuana.

It was also in the twenties that marijuana—as at that time, it first came to be described when taken for nonmedical purposes—began to acquire a sinister reputation. This was due in part to the stories coming out of Egypt, where hashish was still being blamed for the high addiction rate. At the same time, the use of marijuana began to spread from the South (where it had been used primarily by slaves) to the North—into the states of the Union where it had not been known before.

Federal Controls

At about the same time, the Federal Bureau of Narcotics was established as a wing of the Treasury Department in Washington, D. C. (1930). It moved to have marijuana banned throughout the country. The Treasury Department would not go along with this and issued the following statement:

> A great deal of public interest has been aroused by newspaper articles appearing from time to time on the evils of the abuse

of marijuana, or Indian hemp. This publicity tends to magnify the extent of the evil and lends color to the inference that there is an alarming spread of the improper use of the drug, whereas the actual increase in such use may not have been inordinately large.

Harry Anslinger, first chief of the new narcotics bureau, set out to make the smoking of marijuana a crime of high degree. He was disturbed at the Treasury Department for rejecting his efforts to ban it and when given the power of his new position, he endeavored to use it to get Congress to rule in his favor. Anslinger had been assistant commissioner for Prohibition. According to *The Forbidden Game,* he had a "deep repugnance for drugs dating back, by his own account, to an episode in his childhood. He had been born in Pennsylvania near a township in which one adult out of ten was reported to be an opium addict. As a twelve-year-old, he heard a woman screaming in agony for the drug, a sound he never forgot. He had come to feel the same horror of marijuana."

Anslinger's bureau was successful and in 1937, the Treasury Department introduced a federal marijuana bill, putting the drug into the same category as the hard narcotics controlled by the Harrison Act. Prior to, and immediately following, the passage of the new marijuana law, a flood of materials in the form of pamphlets, booklets, radio broadcasts, and lectures were produced, either directly by Anslinger or by his directive. The bureau chief realized he had to do a better job of controlling the drug than he had been able to do with alcohol. One of the people Anslinger turned to to aid his campaign against marijuana was a "hot gospeller" by the name of Earl Albert Rowell, who had been touring America and lecturing audiences on marijuana's effect.

Rowell's Claims

The drug, according to Rowell's estimations, was evil for the following reasons:

1. Destroys willpower, making a jellyfish of the user. He cannot say no.
2. Eliminates the line between right and wrong.

3. Above all, causes crime, fills the victim with an irrepressible urge to violence.
4. Incites to revolting immorality, including rape and murder.
5. Causes many accidents, both industrial and automotive.
6. Ruins careers forever.
7. Causes insanity as its specialty.
8. Either in self-defense or as a means of revenue, users make smokers of others, thus perpetuating evil.

However, when Rowell tried to link cigarette smoking to pot, Anslinger had to back off. Rowell tried to show cigarette smoking was a stepping-stone to the use of marijuana.

Varying State Laws

I cite the above bit of history to show how and why marijuana has been so surrounded by controversy. The confusion is further demonstrated by the wide variance among the states on the penalties for possession and the use of marijuana. The laws also reveal that those who sought to link marijuana with heroin and other dangerous drugs succeeded. For example, in Alabama, a second conviction for any possession of grass can bring up to forty years in prison and a $25,000 fine. In Arizona, where at one time possession of one ounce of marijuana could get you life imprisonment, the law now calls for possession of any amount of grass to be prosecuted as a felony. At the same time, the exact same amount resulted in a $20 fine in the state of South Dakota.

In spite of this, it became obvious by the sixties that the campaign to stamp out marijuana was not succeeding. After it surfaced among the beat generation of the fifties and the hippies of the sixties, the habit spread rapidly throughout the country. Until recently, its control was primarily by law enforcement. In 1960, there were 169 arrests in connection with marijuana in the state of Connecticut, but by 1965 there were 7,000 arrests, and in 1966, as its middle-class use spread, there were 15,000 arrests.

In the seventies, public attention began changing toward marijuana and drugs in general, in part due to the vast number of users. The police were willing enough to make raids in hippie camps, but did not relish the idea of making sweeps through the massed ranks of fans at pop festivals. Even less appealing was raiding homes of the GIs—sometimes officers—who had brought the habit back with them from Viet Nam.

Politicians, too, could no longer be sure that a hard line on drugs would win them electoral support. In the winter of 1972, the Consumers' Union pronounced that "marijuana is here to stay. No conceivable law enforcement can curb its availability."

In 1973, Oregon took a tentative step toward legislation by converting possession of small quantities of marijuana into a violation comparable to a parking offense. While other states have not gone so far in softening their marijuana laws, many have liberalized them.

Using "Reefer Madness" to Protect Pot

The proponents and promoters for decriminalized and legalized marijuana are using what I call "reefer madness" to their advantage. There has been a slow, subtle, effective campaign—both organized and unorganized—over the past ten years, taking advantage of the controversy surrounding marijuana's confusing laws, medical findings, and unrealistic efforts to stamp it out. The goal is to dupe the American public into accepting marijuana as *a harmless recreational drug.*

The marijuana campaigners have used the media effectively to promote their cause. Just as the news media was used effectively during the forties, fifties, and sixties to feed the public both factual and inaccurate information about drugs, so now marijuana's Madison Avenue-type promoters are using the media to counteract past inaccuracies. In addition, they have also managed to pull off a cover-up of sorts regarding the most recent findings on its dangers. Thus, marijuana proponents have had a favorable press, while the research and warnings against it have either gone unprinted or been hidden in the back pages of the newspaper.

For example, when television star Mary Tyler Moore made an offhand remark in which she stated, "I've tried marijuana and consider it to be less harmful than alcohol," her picture made front-page news. The result: Millions of kids read it with pleasure. Those looking for reasons that they should not worry about its harm are thereby reinforced in their prejudices. And Ms. Moore is made to look like an authority after a few puffs on pot. Later the same evening, Johnny Carson of the NBC "Tonight" show made a point to call attention to her propot remark with a smile on his face, as if to say if good and wholesome Mary Tyler Moore smokes pot, it must not be all that bad. But when a doctor or medical research team uncovers data that indicates marijuana to be harmful to the body, it is unlikely to make either front or back page of the same paper. One must discover it in a medical journal.

Public apathy and public opinion have turned promarijuana, and the media have responded accordingly. The opinion makers (and the people who influence and finance them) have also joined the ranks of the pot experimenters—and some have become regular users. Maxine Cheshire, in an article in *Family Circle* entitled "Drugs in Washington, D.C." asks the question: "Do pot, cocaine and more dangerous drugs influence our highest decision makers and those close to them?" The article goes on to state:

> In 1978, the social winds continue to blow eastward. Hollywood, bored with alcohol and publicized affairs, has embraced a new high—drugs—and Washington, D.C., is following suit. Many Washington parties serve cocaine and marijuana as naturally as martinis, and insiders suggest that if the total extent of drug abuse in the Capital was exposed, the resulting scandal would touch every area of government— from the hallowed halls of Congress to many a chandeliered embassy and even to the White House. Drugs, particularly the "fashionable ones," have become so acceptable in Washington that even some White House guests feel free to indulge in them, on the premises.
>
> At the White House's first jazz festival on the South Lawn this summer [1978], a haze of marijuana smoke hung heavy under the low-bending branches of a magnolia tree when President Carter darted behind the bandstand to congratulate the musicians. One of the President's bodyguards looked uncomfortable and feebly fanned the air around his boss. But if Carter recognized the aroma that enveloped him, he pretended to notice nothing.

I have been working in the drug-abuse field for over twenty years. I have watched drug use go from the drug pusher's house to the

White House. Fifteen years ago, I (and millions of others) would never have believed this report.

The Drug Revolution and Public Indignation

In the early sixties, drug use was confined to the ghettos and among blacks, Puerto Ricans, Chicanos, and other minority groups. Prior to this period, marijuana was the exclusive indulgence of jazz musicians. It surfaced with the beat generation of the fifties, among poets, artists, and folk musicians. By the late sixties, pot became a new generation's protest drug. A drug revolution spread like wildfire across the country. Kids who previously were protected or isolated from the drug scene were "turning on" and "tuning in."

Paul Dennis and Carolyn Berry, writing in their book *The Marijuana Catalog,* stated: "Marijuana appealed to their [the sixties generation] sense of life's possibilities and helped unify the generation widely diverse in its opinions and interests. The use of marijuana—a sort of 'exclusive' habit—gave the new generation a sense of community and shared values. Even the way it was smoked, passed around in a circle, symbolized the communal experience."

From pot, middle- and upper-class students began popping pills, dropping acid, LSD, speed, and other hallucinogenic drugs—even mainlining heroin. And a previously apathetic society was shaken to its WASPy core. When it was the blacks, Hispanic Americans, and minorities abusing drugs, the rest of the country didn't care. But when it broke out in middle America, drug raids in high schools and colleges were common. Every major newspaper and national magazine carried exposés on the drug scene. Taxpayers clamored for the federal, state, and local governments to do something. Drug treatment and prevention organizations launched a multitude of programs, spending the millions of dollars legislators began to allot for controlling the epidemic of narcotic abuse and addiction. America was on an antidrug and antimarijuana bandwagon.

Change in Attitude Today

That has all changed now. It was only a short time after the earlier mentioned White House jazz festival that Special Assistant to the President for Health Issues, Dr. Peter G. Bourne, resigned when it was alleged he was using recreational drugs (which he denied).

Following the incident, President Carter issued a warning to White House staff workers that he expected everyone to obey the law and anyone using drugs illegally would be fired. "Whether you agree with the law or not is totally irrelevant. . . . You will obey it or you will seek employment elsewhere."

Maxine Cheshire, in her article "Drugs in Washington, D.C.," stated: "The sad truth is that drugs, on the Washington social scene, are 'in.' They are trendy, kicky, chic."

Drugs in Sports

Washington and Hollywood are not the only places in social society that have changed in respect to drugs. So have the gridiron, diamond, and court. I refer to football, baseball, and tennis. Drugs have hit the college and professional (as well as high school) sports realm.

As I write this material, the football world is rocked and shocked with revelations of the widespread use of drugs by NFL players. "Reefer madness" and "cocaine craziness" threaten to damage both the reputation and stability of professional sports, in addition to shattering the idols of millions of fans.

Bobby Cox, the Toronto Blue Jays' manager, stated, "If more than 50% of people 20–35 have tried marijuana, then I guess I'd be kidding myself if I didn't think more than 50% of my players had tried it too."

Harry Edwards, West Coast sociology professor and black athletes' guru (as told to the *Chicago Sun-Times* columnist John Schulian) stated:

> Drugs is our next big catastrophe [in sports] and we're moving towards it right now. When I visit a campus and ask athletes how many of them use dope, they just laugh . . . they think, it's only squares who won't smoke a joint. . . . By 1985, professional sports are going to be drafting 65 to 75% drug users. White kids as well as black kids, suburban kids as well as ghetto kids. Kids using marijuana, cocaine, heroin . . . .

Professional football linebacker Thomas Henderson, a confessed heavy drug user, who began as a teenager with his neighborhood buddies, then graduated to a twelve-hundred-dollar-a-day cocaine-free-basing habit, stated: "Most young adults who have used illicit drugs began with marijuana. About half of those who began with marijuana later tried cocaine and/or other hallucinogens.

"I started with marijuana . . . then it was mainly cocaine," Henderson said. "But, also there were acids . . . everything."

Carl Eller, one time all-pro defensive end for the Minnesota Vikings, who admits to a one-time cocaine habit, estimates that 15 percent of the NFL's 1,500 players are "problem users"—approximately 225 players.

Drugs in the Work Place

Reefer madness has also spread to the factory, office, and business world.

In the U.S. Dept. of Health and Human Services Bulletin Prevention Resources (Winter 1981), it declares in an article entitled "The Work Place as a Setting for Drug-Abuse Prevention":

> Several studies of drugs in the work place bore out the fact that employees at every level of business and industry were among those who used and abused a wide variety of chemical substances. One of the studies published in 1970, conducted for the Research Institute of America, showed that, in the New York City area, 90% of the company surveys reported incidents of drug abuse on their premises, increased absenteeism, poor work performance, thefts, higher insurance rates and consequent cost of drug abuse that ran into the millions of dollars. A study conducted for the New York State Narcotic Addiction Control Commission (1971) reported significant rates of record use of drugs in all occupational groups except farmers.
>
> The Conference Board, an independent, nonprofit business research organization, published a report in 1974 indicating that drug abuse had become a problem of 31% of the 800 large companies surveyed. Alcoholism had long been recognized as

a serious problem in the work force—white collar no less than blue—so it was not surprising that the Conference Board study showed that alcoholism among employees was a problem in 70% of the companies surveyed. Drug abuse was found to be most prevalent in companies located in or employing most of their work force in cities of 100,000 population or more.

In 1975 the U.S. military forces, a major employer, estimated the cost of lost production in the military because of alcoholism and drug abuse was over $400 million.

What brought about this change in the middle- and upper-class attitude towards drugs—the very drugs which are now inflicting serious damage in government, industry, sports, the military, and so forth? Why have we, within a relatively short period, gone from an antipot society to propot? Why have the *bad guys* of the sixties become the *in guys* of the eighties? Why has the call gone from "lock 'em up" to "let 'em alone"? Whereas "reefer madness" once described an overobsession against the use of marijuana, it now describes society's obsession and embracing of it.

Reasons for Attitude Change

I propose there are a number of reasons for this about-face in our drug attitudes:

Past efforts to warn kids about drugs contain too many myths, half-truths and false information. Marijuana, for example, was lumped in among all the rest of the dangerous drugs. Pot was thought to be a lead-in or stepping-stone to other more potent and dangerous drugs, and it was the beginning drug for the hard-core users in the late fifties and early sixties. Marijuana was, at the time, part and parcel of the whole gamut of narcotics available on the streets. The route from grass to junk was short, easy, and inevitable. Marijuana and heroin were rarely used exclusively of each other.

But then something happened to separate marijuana and the other soft drugs from the hard ones. Speed, LSD, STP, pills, and heroin became the experimental drugs of the middle-class in the early seventies. Many became hooked—hard-core junkies. They were no different from the Harlem or ghetto-street junkies. This shook our nation to its core. A massive drug-education campaign swept the country. Kids realized, in time, that the hard stuff was a monkey on their backs that they could not get rid of. Adults did all they could to deter all drug use. But in the zeal and desperation to turn kids away from dope, marijuana was lumped in with all drugs—but the users knew differently. Drug use became more sophisticated. Young people learned (some, the hard way) that heroin was physically addicting but marijuana was not. Thus, many drug-education and prevention programs lost credibility with the kids. Young people smoked pot either out of protest or because they knew it was safer than the hallucinogenics and heroin. Marijuana, among middle-class youth, became primarily a recreational drug, while in the poorer areas it continued to be the lead-in drug to the more dangerous stuff.

Marijuana became the "lesser evil by comparison" drug. Because all the attention was focused on prevention, controlling, and treating the hard-core users, and because the myths surrounding marijuana were finally exposed, it ended up the drug of choice of the majority of young people who wanted to experiment with drugs but not go to the extent of the street junkie. "Pot is not addicting," the kids would say in justification or defense of their smoking grass. "It's no worse than alcohol" was and is the other popular argument. Therefore, I believe marijuana has won popularity by default. It has sneaked in, so to speak, while the country was worrying about and chasing the pusher and heroin junkies. Unfortunately while liberalizing marijuana laws because of this "lesser evil by comparison" method, no one was examining the dangers of marijuana on its own merits. Naturally, marijuana comes out the innocent party when compared with LSD, speed, heroin, and other types of hard drugs. But marijuana needs no comparison. It is a drug. *It must be analyzed on its own.* Why we have allowed the proponents of marijuana to launch their campaign to decriminalize it without challenge or investigation into its prolonged effects on regular users is a mystery. *The idea that marijuana is harmless is a great American hoax.*

Drugs have reached the upper crust. From Hollywood to Washington, D.C., pot (and now cocaine) is becoming as common as booze and broken marriages. Or, as has been stated, drugs are consumed as freely as hors d'oeuvres.

"It's not possible to have a party without someone using drugs," say some hostesses.

In fact, pot smoking among stars and upper-class professionals is so common in some places that it's not even given a second thought. Many celebrities are turning on with "coke" (cocaine) for various reasons. In addition to using it as a party pleasure, some are using it during work—even taking it before a game show or talk program, claiming it intensifies their reactions and kills on-camera jitters. Mike Douglas claims that some of his guest stars come on the program stoned.

David Toma writes:

> Too many of their [youth] media idols use dope and don't keep it a secret. I mean stars like the Rolling Stones and Paul McCartney. You could fill a telephone directory with their names. Rock concerts are drug events and nobody seems to give a damn. Hip movies like Cheech & Chong's *Up in Smoke* glorified drugs and so do T.V. shows like "Saturday Night Live." Everybody seems to be doing it and having fun and the anti-drug voices are so soft and tentative that they can't be heard.

Jan Goodwin, writing in *Family Circle* magazine, asks the question, "Can drugs affect government decisions?" She further writes:

> The broad social effect of drug taking by performers and theatrical celebrities can best be measured in the permissive climate it creates and the example it sets for young people. But when officials at government level are involved, a whole new set of questions arise. Are important decisions being clouded by "recreational" chemicals? Are governments endorsing drug use by "looking the other way"? Is illegality the only reason for disciplining elected public officials and government employees who are known to be drug users?

What is most disturbing about the celebrity drug users is the influence they have over youthful fans. They become very poor models. Couple this with a few key Washington officials, either outrightly condoning marijuana use or giving tacit approval of it, and no wonder 55 million or more Americans have experimented with pot.

America has lost the war on drugs. We've lost the war on drugs because we've lost the will to fight against them anymore. Other problems are draining the energy and the pocketbooks of the taxpayers. In addition, the failure of most of the past rehabilitation programs has turned the public away from its previously declared war on narcotics.

History bears out that when our nation cannot control the vices of the citizenry, we end up legalizing our habits in order to get the tax dollar out of them. We are very near doing this with marijuana. Technically, we have not legalized heroin but the government has thrown in the towel, in effect, trying to rehabilitate the hard-core addicts. The number-one drug pushers in America are the federal and state government drug agencies that dispense methadone. They thus end up perpetuating the addicts' addiction.

"We must accept the fact that heroin addicts have a disease. We must give them methadone in the same manner that diabetics must take insulin," one official stated. Drug abuse no longer stirs the emotions of Americans as it once did. We have come to believe that drugs, especially marijuana, are like alcohol—that they're here to stay. Some of the very same people who in past days stood up against the abuse of drugs now condone marijuana, embrace it, and smoke it.

Marijuana has become so pervasive in our society that some hostesses will even offer it to their guests as casually as they offer after-dinner mints and coffee. Books and magazines that advocate drugs-for-fun can be found in most bookstores or on the neighborhood drugstore magazine rack.

"Society is giving kids the message that pot is okay," says Dr. Mitchell Rosenthal, president of Phoenix House, the country's largest residential drug-treatment center. "By sitting back and doing nothing, parents allow kids to think drugs are harmless."

One factor that has also changed is in the drug itself. Colombian-cultivated marijuana is now the prevailing street-level pot in use. It is stronger, on an average, by ten times than the marijuana that had been available over the past years. This is why the air and seaways are crowded with new-type smugglers, taking advantage not only of official and unofficial tolerance toward marijuana smoking, but cashing in on the more potent quality of the Colombian hemp plant.

3
The Colombian... Cuban... Californian Connections

Tens of thousands of pounds of South American (Colombian) "gold" marijuana makes its way (some by way of Cuba) into the lungs of the estimated 50 to 60 million Americans who have tried pot. The total street value of drugs in the U.S. (according to a 1980 National Narcotics Intelligence Consumer Committee study) is $68.5 billion to $90 billion. Of this amount, marijuana's annual street-sale value is approximately 40 percent of this total—$18.3 billion to $26.8 billion.

Until recently 80 percent of the marijuana crop came from Colombia, which has been to the pot smoker what the French Connection was to the heroin user. The manufacture and distribution of illegal drugs is one of the biggest worldwide industries.

Colombia Still Tops

Now there is the "Californian Connection." American growers, not only in California (which is believed to be the state with the largest amount of homegrown pot), but in almost every state are now rivaling the Colombian grown and smuggled marijuana.

Colombia is still the ideal country for growing marijuana, known there as *Santa Marta gold.* Because of the favorable soil conditions, an ideal Andes climate, and an ideal shoreline of regular terrain, this part of South America is the marijuana grower's paradise. There are approximately 250,000 acres of cultivated land available for growing the plant. It has made this small South American country the world's drug provider.

One U.S. drug enforcement administration agent stated: "It's a trafficker's paradise. Colombia is the largest supplier of marijuana in the world."

With the unofficial approval of Colombian authorities, the growers, sellers, exporters, and dealers give the country a combined total of smuggling profits of over $3 billion per year—$700 million more than all the country's legal exports. Some prominent figures have suggested that the incredibly profitable drug market might well be institutionalized in the near future.

The Colombian fields have a potential of producing 6 billion pounds of marijuana annually. Each pound is worth anywhere from $600 to $1200 on American streets, depending on the class of the market where it's sold. With this vast supply, it is no wonder that ships, planes, and commercial air travelers have established smuggling routes from Bogota to New York, Chicago, and Los Angeles. In between the 5000 miles is a network of farmers, smugglers, brokers, and fixers—all getting a cut of the action, including Fidel Castro's island empire.

Cuba's Connection

According to a *New York Post* newspaper article (Monday, June 21, 1982), written by Arnaud de Borchgrave and Robert Moss, investigative reporters: "Cuba is an active partner in the drug traffic" coming into the United States "and skims the profits to the tune of tens of billions of dollars a year."

"Fidel Castro's secret service, the D.G.I., orchestrates a drugs-for-arms barter trade between Marxist guerrillas" and the drug lords of Miami, Florida, and Medellin, Colombia.

According to the article the Cubans get their cut by exacting "tolls from dopers who make stopovers in Cuba enroute from Colombia to South Florida and use the receipts to finance undercover operations and to buy arms from dealers in the United States and West Europe—weapons that are shipped clandestinely to guerrillas in South America."

In addition, alleged American-made weapons have also been purchased and warehoused in the Florida area until they could be safely transported to Colombia. The vast amounts of money the Cubans could make by serving as a safe haven for traffickers—providing fuel, repairing boats, and so forth—brought about this new "Cuban Connection" between Colombia and the United States, primarily South Florida.

A July 1982 *Reader's Digest* article entitled "Havana's Drug-Smuggling Connection" gives this report: "Until the mid-1970s, Colombian smugglers shipped millions of tons of marijuana and cocaine to the U.S. without the aid of the Cuban government." And, in fact, the smugglers had to carefully navigate their ships and boats through the Windward Passage, a narrow strip of water between the eastern tip of Cuba and Haiti. "The smallest error in navigation, however, could place a vessel within Cuban waters, where it would be seized, its cargo of drugs confiscated and crew imprisoned."

In late 1975, however, a deal was struck between major smugglers and the Cuban government. Safe passage would be provided the smugglers, even a safe port in return for a fee. The *Reader's Digest* article states: "It was an offer the smugglers could not refuse. Even a modest 25-ton marijuana shipment could bring its owners as much as $12 million when off-loaded to American importers. Thus, $800,000 [payoff] was simply a business expense. For Havana, the arrangement provided cash for Marxist insurgencies under way in Nicaragua, El Salvador and Guatemala. And the smugglers who carry drugs north could ferry supplies and weapons for guerrilla forces on their trip back."

Through this unique linkup of the Colombian, Cuban, United States "connections," what is really meant is that unknowingly when a youth in Eldred, New York (or thousands of other little towns, villages, as well as big cities), buys and smokes a joint, he is helping to finance the spread of communism and guerrilla warfare in Central America.

Estimate of the amount of illegal drugs coming into South Florida alone is $7 billion a year, according to one report.

High Profits Draw "Businessmen"

With such high profits at stake, it is no surprise that so many novices and small-time entrepreneurs, as well as wealthy businessmen, using legitimate fronts, are risking their efforts, as well as arrest, to cash in on such a tax-free growth industry. For example, a police chief in one city was indicted for smuggling pot. A New Orleans business executive was charged with trafficking 185 tons of marijuana. A millionaire rancher was caught using shrimp boats to ship pot into this country. In Tennessee, a forty-year-old grocer was indicted on illegal smuggling of marijuana.

A special FBI agent stated that "some of the community's most upright citizens, including doctors, lawyers and businessmen, were providing seed money for narcotics smuggling. Many of these 'good, solid citizens'," said the agent, "were attracted to the business by the rate of return as high as 25 percent a week, but others were victims of extortion through prostitution."

A 1979 murder of District Judge John H. Wood, Jr. demonstrates the seriousness of the drug business. *Judge Wood was the first federal judge to be murdered in more than a century. His slaying is believed to have been the result of his hard line against convicted drug smugglers.* The New York Times called Judge Wood "a merciless enemy of drug traffickers. He assessed the maximum of legal penalty in 72 of his 90 narcotic cases that ended in convictions."

Since 1974, marijuana consumption has quadrupled, which is no doubt the reason for the rush to cash in on the lucrative market. *Time* magazine (January 29, 1979) stated: "The big money in the Colombian drug operation goes not to those who grow narcotics or process them but to those who get them to the American consumers. One way to get the drugs out is to supply them from one of the hundreds of clandestine airstrips that have been bulldozed in the Guajira Peninsula [of Colombia]."

The Crowded Airlanes

There are an estimated 800 airstrips on the Guajira Peninsula. There may be as many in Florida as well as in the southeast and southwestern portions of the United States. Some landings have been accomplished by using the headlight beams of two pickup trucks to sight the landing strip on secluded flat land, thus avoiding radar detection and making it difficult for investigators to detect.

One daredevil pilot, who according to his calculation, had made nearly 130 runs, gave an interview to *High Times*. (This magazine is directed to the pot generation and its very existence and success is yet another indication of a widespread popularity in the usage of marijuana.) The airman stated: "The pot lanes are busier than the commercial routes over Palm Beach Airport. I've seen planes lined up for hours waiting to land. The situation is really dangerous. There have probably been mid-air collisions."

He was asked, "How much do you make?"

"About $10 a pound.... There is no Mr. Big. If you take 6,000 pounds, there's probably 600 people involved in it by the time it gets down to the street."

With the possibility of making $25,000 to $50,000 in a 24-hour period, it is no wonder pilots are in plenty. Again, this is all of course tax free—a part of an overall illegal "underground" economy estimated at $450 to $470 million a year in transactions.

Some pilots and planes have been lost at sea. With the rush to cash in on the lucrative business, poorly serviced engines and marginally safe planes are not uncommon; yet the high "payoff" spurs the smuggler on in spite of some risks. The Colombian military, in an apparent public display to show some government control of the situation, reportedly seized some drug-laden craft. In actuality, however, the Colombian government seems to be a part of the drug-smuggling trade. Two U.S. customs agents visiting in Colombia to talk with government authorities about getting cooperation between our two countries were shot and killed.

A sister industry, airplane brokering, has also sprung up as a result of the large numbers of airplanes involved in smuggling. The brokers are not usually involved in the actual drug trafficking (though they occasionally may be) but provide the smugglers with lease-and-lend wings, equipped with the extra fuel tank necessary for making the long flight back and forth across the Caribbean. Fake corporate documents often make it impossible for the authorities to trace the ownership or even the identity of the aircraft.

"There had been times when we had the airplane and the dope physically in our hands and were not able to find out who owned it," said an agent of the Federal Drug Enforcement Administration.

Also by Sea

The daily supply of pot for the American street buyer comes not only by plane. As mentioned before, ship smugglers are carrying the profitable cargo from Latin America to the New York area and other major distribution points, embarking either in South Florida or other ports of call along the East Coast. Small, flagless freighters brought out of mothballs (or those ready for the scrap yard), have been put into service for an organized crime group, according to federal law-enforcement officials.

This shipping is now a multimillion-dollar operation and because of the sudden rise of marijuana use beginning in the early seventies, officials believe a major organized-crime faction decided to expand into the major trafficking trade. This is why and how Fidel Castro and the "Cuban Connection" was initiated.

Pot Farmers

The newest marijuana "connection" lies possibly in our backyard, the neighbors' or out of town in some rural farmland. An October 12, 1981, *U.S. News & World Report* article "Marijuana: a U.S. Farm Crop That's Booming" states: "All across America, furtive farmers are racing early frosts and police raids to bring in a record harvest of what is rapidly turning into a major cash crop—marijuana.

"Amounts of the illegal weed already seized and destroyed in raids over recent weeks have convinced law-enforcement officials that pot farming is a multibillion-dollar national industry."

The article goes on to report that marijuana is being grown commercially in 43 of California's 58 counties, with unofficial estimates of its worth put at approximately $1 billion. Thus it rivals the grape crop and is twice as valuable as the raisin harvest. Authorities have found marijuana growing between the California grapevines.

In addition, thousands of pot smokers are growing the plant in backyards, on windowsills or in greenhouses for personal use. NORML (National Organization for the Reform of Marijuana Laws) estimates that 1 million people grow small amounts for personal use and up to 100,000 do so for profit. (The actual amount is, no doubt, smaller than this, as NORML makes it a practice to overinflate any and all figures relative to marijuana smoking or growing, in order to give the impression that "everybody is doing it.") However, there is no doubt that the new American marijuana "connection" is a growing problem.

"The logistics are a lot easier," explains E. Wayne Dickey. Quoted in the *U.S. News & World Report* article, this agent with the Florida Department of Law Enforcement declared: "It's easier than going to Colombia, making a deal and hoping you'll get out of there alive." Authorities estimate that in Florida alone the marijuana crop is grossing approximately $400 million a year, second only to the orange crop.

Effectiveness of Enforcement

How effective are the efforts to stop the Colombian, Cuban, Californian or other U.S. "connections"?

Until recently, it was estimated that only about 10 percent of all the illegal drugs coming into the United States was being intercepted. Smugglers had gotten so bold, they hardly bothered to hide their activities.

The Reagan administration, however, stepped up enforcement and seizure activities. Vice-president Bush was sent to Florida in 1982 to highlight the government's new plan and "Task Force" to combat crime, immigration problems, and especially drug smuggling in South Florida. Bush announced the assignment of 145 new custom agents, 43 additional FBI agents and 58 new DEA (Drug Enforcement Agency), plus other support personnel. In addition, the administration gave this Task Force the unprecedented access to military assistance by getting a law through Congress to allow the armed forces to get involved in this war against drug smuggling. Beginning in the fall of 1981—in a campaign code-named Operation Thunderbolt—U.S. Navy E2-C Hawkeye radar planes and Cobra helicopters were pressed into service to identify and chase down smuggling planes. The E2-C is capable of spotting anything in the air within a 200 to 300 mile radius and can spot a floating buoy from 30,000 feet up. Also for the first time, navy vessels, so far only identified as "warships," are patrolling the Caribbean in search of smuggling ships. They carry teams of trained custom agents who do the actual busting.

The Colombian... Cuban... Californian Connections

How effective has this new military-civilian war against drug smuggling been? Apparently successful enough to have the editors of *High Times,* the dope user's major source of drug information, concerned. In a July 1982 *High Times* magazine article in a section called *"High Witness News,"* it is admitted that "cocaine and marijuana shortages could produce moderate price increases if the Task Force manages to seize an unusually large portion of the shipments bound for our shores."

A number of large and dramatic seizures have been made as a result of this Task Force. One such raid confiscated $4 billion worth of drugs.

In March 1982, shortly after the U.S. Customs Tactical Enforcement Team (TEST) had gotten off the ground, a routine inspection of a cargo plane just in from Medellin, Colombia, came surprisingly upon a stash in awesome proportions. They found, packed in 21 boxes supposedly containing clothing, approximately 4,000 pounds of fresh flake (cocaine). This was nearly five times as much cocaine as had ever been taken previously in a single haul.

On another occasion, 6.4 million tons of marijuana were seized, estimated to be one-fifth of all such drug traffic coming from Colombia.

Does this mean we will soon see less marijuana in use? Not likely! The demand seems too great. And public apathy towards drugs, particularly marijuana, is a further reason the law enforcement efforts have been too little and too late. Mr. Ralph Salerno, a former New York City police lieutenant and an expert on organized crime affairs stated: "There's big money in marijuana now and even the image of selling pot isn't bad for the mob. They're not hooking ghetto kids on heroin. Instead, they're providing a commodity for college students and the middle-class."

Peter Bensinger, former head of DEA said: "Our [seizures] efforts are so uphill that it is more than a challenge. The public attitude must change about drugs so the profitability for traffickers will decrease."

Pot's New Industry

While the public turns away or tolerates the smokers, tokers, small- and big-time distributors, another industry has sprung up called the "paraphernalia industry." Three billion dollars a year is spent on such things as Smoke Scope (a pipe for smoking pot), supergrass (a process for growing marijuana), high roller (for rolling cigarettes), *Cannabis indica* (paper made from a blend of plants on Turkish, Pakistani, and Indian plantations).

The pot culture can locate paraphernalia in magazines such as *Hilife* and *High Times*. The latter claims to have over four million readers. Another magazine, *Stone Age,* boldly advertises itself as "the all-new dope magazine ... the lavish new magazine by dopers, for dopers. It's about your favorite leisure activities—pot, hash, coke, LSD and psilocybin and a host of other natural highs."

Such periodicals also carry market quotations of marijuana from Afghanistan to Hawaii. Qualities are listed from "good" to "knockout"—with a list of prices on each.

The same paraphernalia can also be purchased in "head shops," which have sprung up all across the country.

It is obvious from all of this that marijuana is much more widespread than anyone can imagine. A multimillion-dollar industry has sprung up under our noses. It is so far out of hand, with so many people, countries, and products involved that it would be virtually impossible to stop it without creating a new prohibition. Edward M. Brecher stated, in a Consumer's Union report on marijuana drug policies entitled *Licit and Illicit Drugs:* "It is now much too late to debate the issue: marijuana versus no marijuana. Marijuana is here to stay. No conceivable law-enforcement policy can curb its availability."

The Colombian, Cuban, and Californian connections are well oiled. The routes are working like clockwork. The government agencies and law-enforcement people responsible to stop the drug industry need more money and power and manpower to do anything more than make periodic seizures. For each ship stopped or aircraft grounded, there are many more to take its place. And in spite of big headlines about key pushers being arrested in large cities, and tons of marijuana and other drugs being confiscated, the traffickers continue to smuggle dope into the country and our youth continue to "go up in smoke."

4
Grass Roots

An estimated 40 million Americans smoke marijuana at least once a month.

In all, an estimated 68 million Americans—teenagers, even eight to twelve-year-olds, young adults, white- and blue-collar workers, professionals, doctors, lawyers, and so forth—have experimented with "grass."

Of the 40 million who smoke pot, more than half are believed to be regular users (several times a week).

According to the NBC report "Reading, Writing, and Reefers," nearly 5 million of the above "cop a buzz"—a term chronic abusers use to describe the "high" they get from a joint.

Who are the "grass roots" users?
Why do they smoke?
What do they think about marijuana?
How does it affect them?
How often and how much do the potheads smoke?
Has drug abuse peaked?

"We've gone through a period of approximately 20 years during which there was dramatic increase in the use of drugs in this country," according to psychiatrist William Pollin, Director of NIDA (National Institute of Drug Abuse). "In most health and social problem fields, if you get a 20 to 50% increase—that's dramatic. If you get 100% increase, that's epidemic. In the area of drug abuse, we had a *3000% increase.*"

For the first time in seventeen years, the use of narcotics by teenagers leveled off in 1980. But the question must be asked—at what peak has it leveled and at what price to the abusers?

Effect of Decriminalization Laws

This 3000 percent twenty-year rise in drug abuse is a direct result of the decriminalization laws. Before decriminalization, I asked a university student why he did not smoke pot. He said, "Not because I don't want to. But the risk is too great. I don't want to blow a four-year education and a future career on a few joints."

Today, the same type of student doesn't have to worry about the law or the authorities. In many cases, the law has been changed or ignored.

A 1979 statewide survey by the New York State Division of Substance Abuse Service of a projected half million full-time undergraduate college students showed that the drugs most frequently used in the past six months—termed "recent" use—were:

- *Marijuana*—used by 59 percent or 291,000 students
- *Hashish*—used by 28 percent or 138,000 students
- *Stimulants*—used by 21 percent or 103,000 students
- *Cocaine*—used by 20 percent or 101,000 students

"We have always considered college students a group at particular risk for substance abuse," said division director Julio A. Martinez. "The survey results are alarming, even for a group believed to be widely involved with drugs. For instance, the figures show that more college students smoke marijuana than smoke cigarettes," he said. In another drug-use survey, it found 27 percent who said they had smoked pot "in the past week." Sixty-five percent among all students surveyed confessed to smoking marijuana, whereas in 1967 a similar survey found only 5 percent users; in 1974 53 percent said they had smoked it.

As a Harvard University sophomore commented, "Marijuana use is virtually universal. It's as social an activity as drinking."

More Smokers Are Younger

Since the above surveys were made what is most alarming is the rise of drug use, marijuana again in particular, among high-school and junior high-school students. Pot smoking which began among way-out bohemian-type-young adults in the fifties, then spread to hippie-types in the sixties to college students in the seventies and has now infiltrated the high-school campus—even elementary age children.

In *The Private Life of the American Teenager* by Jane Norman

Grass Roots

and Myron Harris, Ph.D., the authors surveyed over 160,000 young people. On matters of drug use among the teenagers who responded to their questionnaire they found:

- Forty percent of teenagers smoke marijuana *regularly*
- Seven out of ten high school teenagers have tried marijuana
- Fifty percent will lie to parents about their pot use

In another survey, reported in the magazine *Your Place,* 1,721 respondents filled out a questionnaire telling when and why they "go to pot." Ninety-four percent said they had smoked pot at one time or another. The survey confirmed other studies which show that the younger one begins smoking, the more likely he is to smoke regularly in later life.

About one-fourth of all current marijuana smokers are under seventeen. There is also evidence that a portion of them (about 5 percent) are twelve- or thirteen-year-olds. One teenage pot smoker, a chronic user, began at the age of eight. "My brother gave it to me when he and his friends baby-sat me," he said. By the age of twelve, he was an admitted pothead.

Tragically, many youthful users are becoming more than occasional experimenters. Chronic use is on the upswing, creating a class of pot smokers called "chronic abusers." This high increase of teenage and preteen abuse of marijuana is a direct result of the decriminalization laws. Kids from middle- and upper-class homes have easy access to pot among classmates, even inside the school. Its use is no longer among a fringe group. The most popular, intellectual, even athletic types—who in the past would never have been abusers of drugs or marijuana—are now smokers and tokers.

Stronger Stuff

Another reason for extensive use of marijuana and marijuana dependence, particularly among chronic users, has come about because of a stronger type of marijuana in circulation. Forrest Tennant, M.D., who is Director of Community Health Services in West Covina, California, and an advisory board member of the National Anti-Drug Coalition, stated in the magazine *War on Drugs:*

Looking at the NIDA studies done in high schools throughout the United States and seeing that about 10% of teenagers use it over 20 times a month, I think that we may have to assume that as much as at least 5% of high-school kids may be terribly dependent on marijuana right now and can't stop. That's my guess; I should say, an educated guess. But we have no hard factual data on this.

Another point we should make is that one of the reasons, I believe, why many people in this country have thought marijuana was harmless was that they've always had very weak marijuana in the United States, averaging one or two percent T.H.C. content. In the late 1960's and early 1970's, both in Europe as well as in Vietnam, with American soldiers, we saw them using high-grade marijuana and hashish and we really saw the complications there. That's when I really became very alerted to the problems with this drug.

Another thing that's really caused the tide to turn here is that we're now seeing in the United States high grade marijuana and hashish from five to fifteen percent T.H.C. content, and those are the people who are really getting into trouble. And that's important for people to understand why the marijuana situation is really coming to the forefront. Not only do we have research showing things, we also have smokers using these high grade forms now which cause them trouble and it's really showing up.

Pot and Teens

Jane Norman and Myron Harris quoted earlier in *The Private Life of the American Teenager* said:

Those who smoke excessively are termed "potheads" and placed in an unfavored category by a majority of their peers. In some circles, those who smoke on the way to school, or outside the school building, are considered potheads by those who seldom or do not smoke at all. However, the definition of excessive use depends on the social circumstances of the school and the peer group. The term pothead may be used as one of criticism or derision in a school where pot is rarely used. In another school or setting where heavy pot smoking is the norm, pothead may be used affectionately by peers to denote "one of the gang."

The writers found "seven out of ten teenagers" smoke pot by the age of sixteen to eighteen and "Even by the age of 15, 42% have experimented. Marijuana use crosses every racial, age, sex and socioeconomic line."

Most kids smoke pot because it makes them feel good. Curiosity is usually the reason they try it in the first place. The relaxed sensation, the temporary feeling of escape from boredom, depression ("or just being down"), as well as worry about school, home, or personal problems lead to further use.

Most pot smoking is associated with "partying," at least at first. A seventeen-year-old told me, "when you smoke pot, it's no fun when you smoke alone. You've got to have someone to talk to—unless you like to talk to yourself. You always talk to people when you smoke pot. Then we always laughed and looked for trouble."

A list of reasons kids give for smoking pot are :

- To have a good time—goof off!
- It relaxes me and makes it easier to socialize!
- Negative emotions disappear!
- It blocks out problems!

However within six months of regular pot smoking, its true effects begin to take their toll. The first evidence, among teenagers, is its effect on their ability to concentrate in school, in the classroom, or when doing homework.

Mike, a former user of LSD, pills, and other mind-bending drugs, began smoking pot at the age of fourteen. He moved quickly from use to abuse—smoking several joints a day. "I got high the first couple times and then I just did it as much as I could. It seemed one of the goals back then was to see how long and how high you could stay," Mike stated.

How did it affect him? "At first I used to feel it would make me more intense. In everything I was doing, I felt I could do it better when I was high with marijuana," he explained.

"Like a ... if you played sports or drove a car or whatever, you'd think you were doing it a lot better than if you were straight. I would feel more bold and I would do things I felt I could get away with."

But eventually Mike could not fool himself anymore. It began to affect his schoolwork. "I couldn't concentrate," he said. "I'd be in another world just drifting. It's like you weren't even a part of the classroom. As a result, my grades went straight downhill." He passed eleventh grade by his own admission "by the skin of my teeth." Then he dropped out. Pot did him in, as far as school is concerned.

A young teenager interviewed by news commentator Edwin Newman on the NBC news special "Reading, Writing, and Reefers" confessed that he smoked "about one hundred joints a week" or on an average, a little over ten a day.

Asked how many in school were on pot, he stated: "Only about 20% don't."

Al, another sixteen-year-old from a white, affluent neighborhood, said about his pot smoking: "I smoke mostly after school but sometimes a group of us get together during school hours and share a joint. Occasionally, I'll cop a buzz on the way to school. I average about fifty to sixty joints a week, except when I go to a party. Then me and my friends will go through a whole bag." When asked if marijuana caused him to miss school, he revealed: "I've missed about ten to twelve days this term already."

Al is not a member of a street gang. He is not poor. His parents are professional people, and he has the ability to get good grades. But his life is increasingly centered around pot. Tragically, Al is typical of a new generation of habitual marijuana smokers, and he is one reason that it is time to take another look at our drug laws and drug attitudes. We are growing a generation of potheads. These young people are becoming psychologically addicted to marijuana and getting burned out.

Burned Out

"Burned out" is a term applied to chronic users who, because of extensive marijuana smoking, are no longer feeling the same effects from it. They have built up a psychological tolerance to it in their system. It may take them longer to get high and they, in fact, may not even experience the normal high they once did. In other words, they are psychologically addicted. Instead of "copping a buzz" after one joint, it may take two or three—or even more.

Under normal conditions, users state they experience "a nice feeling" or that "they feel relaxed."

"I like to listen to music," said one.

"I like to talk, yeah—talk a lot," said another smoker.

"My buzz lasts for about one hour."

But the feeling and the effect changes for the long-term user. "I noticed," said one pothead, "that I wouldn't be myself anymore and I couldn't remember. People would say things to me, but I could not remember what was said."

Another revealed, "I don't do anything when I'm stoned. I am less aware. I feel drowsy. If I'm stoned in school, I may fall asleep in class."

While I was talking to a group of present and former drug abusers (some had been confirmed addicts), they gave me the following comments about their use and abuse of marijuana and how it affected them:

"It makes you laugh when you don't want to laugh."

"It made me tired, lazy.... Didn't want to do anything!"

"Sometimes I would get into a depressed state."

"Forget things.... I would go to the store to get onions for my mother and bring back rice.... Can't reason."

"Someone would be talking to me and I would drift away.... I was becoming a space cadet, slowly but surely."

"I'd get the 'munchies'—want to eat and eat. I'd finish dinner, smoke pot, then go right to the refrigerator to eat more. This would give me a splitting headache.... Eating also destroys the marijuana's effects and 'brings you down.' I'd go broke eating, smoking, and drinking."

When I asked them if it were possible to get burned out, they all responded immediately in the affirmative. "I needed a bag within a month," one told me. "The high wore off so I started to put dust [angel dust] on my pot to try and boost it."

"What's going to happen if it's legalized is the kids will run to the pusher to get angel dust or something else, 'cause legal stuff will soon wear off."

What about the nonpsychological effects of marijuana? In listening to this group of drug abusers' comments, they confirmed another aspect of marijuana's danger, which in the long run is often more devastating than the physical or psychological damage. That is, the adverse effect on the user's life-style. Drug abuse can turn a good kid into a bad one. It can turn a mixed-up kid into a disturbed kid. And it can turn a normal youth into a social dropout.

The Pot Life-Style

Someone once wrote: "If all a drug does is kill you, it isn't so bad. It's the quality of life it provides you that should be of most concern."

Dr. Edward R. Bloomquist, in *Marijuana: The Second Trip,* quotes a Dr. Millman on this matter.

> Drugs blunt the pain of physiological conflicts that arise during the age period [adolescence] and postpone problem solving. The result is that such a young person emerges as an immature, drug-dependent, poorly integrated adult.

The risk of marijuana use is compounded in this type of youngster, Dr. Millman noted, because they tend to experiment in their search for relief from psychic discomforts.

A person on marijuana may, for example, view what is normally a minor problem or situation as a major one. Lenny, a sixteen-year-old former pot smoker told me: "I would get paranoia. Walking down the street, I would be constantly looking around, thinking someone was going to run up to me and pop me off and rip me off."

Abuse of marijuana tends to alter one's goals and emotional and social drive. This "amotivational syndrome," as it is called, causes long-term users to become preoccupied with pleasure. Dr. D. Harvey Powelson, in private psychiatric practice in Berkeley, California, stated in a pamphlet entitled "Our Most Dangerous Drug" and here reprinted from *Listen* magazine:

> There's no question that people who use marijuana over a significant period of time are clearly in a state of not being interested in anything but feeling good. There are physiological explanations for that.
>
> Marijuana contains a chemical which affects the pleasure center. You get the illusion of feeling good. Then this illusion becomes more important than really feeling good. At the same time, the effect of the drug is wearing off as you become tolerant of it. So you use more of it. And as that goes on, you either have to use stronger drugs or get another high. But this time the high is going to be a chemical or other false illusion, because you have lost the capacity to feel good in natural ways.
>
> At this stage, in the amotivational syndrome, people lose interest in everything else but the drug. And there are literally thousands of people who are only interested in getting high. They may have shifted from marijuana to heroin. A lot of them are shifting to alcohol and this whole false question about marijuana and alcohol is going down the drain because we're seeing younger and younger alcoholics. First they begin combining the two, then they find out they can get drunker with alcohol than they can with marijuana.

The New York State college drug survey mentioned earlier confirms Dr. Powelson's assertion that marijuana is a gateway drug leading to other drugs or the abuse of a combination of drugs. The survey showed the most popularly used drugs in combination include:

- *Marijuana and alcohol*—used by 43 percent or 206,000 students
- *Marijuana, alcohol, and a third drug*—used by 15 percent or 72,000 students
- *Cocaine and marijuana*—used by 14 percent or 70,000 students.

What the "grass roots" surveys, interviews, and the history of approximately two decades of widespread marijuana use and abuse among the general population of teenagers, preteens and young adults tells us is that marijuana is stunting the emotional and psychological growth of its youthful users and abusers. I have witnessed in the course of over twenty years' work in the drug-abuse field what is truly a sad loss of human potential. When I see promising, bright, likable youths turn into social dropouts who get sidetracked on the road of life by what started out as a few pleasurable puffs on a marijuana joint, I know what the experts mean when they talk about the *amotivational syndrome*. No scientific research can calculate such human and spiritual waste. But a multitude of brokenhearted parents know what this means.

Susan Bromwell, in an article published in *Good Housekeeping* entitled "How I Got My Daughter to Stop Smoking Pot," quoted her daughter's thoughts about her marijuana use: "Pot weakens you. You lose your sense of self. One drugged-out person is like another drugged-out person.... You may think you're getting yourself together with pot, but you're not. You're pulling yourself apart."

The saddest conversations I have ever held have been with parents describing the pain of watching their children turn to a lifestyle that is totally alien to what both the children and the parents ever knew before or ever believed would happen as a result of drug abuse.

"It's like a nightmare, reverend," one father told me. "Let alone what it's doing to my son—look what it's doing to me. I holler and scream at my son. I'm not the same man I used to be. It's killing something inside me. I'll never be the same again.... To think that it all started when our son started hanging out down the street with a group of kids who were smoking pot!"

Pot and Crime

Another sad but dangerous effect that marijuana has on some users is its correlation with crime. In some cases, the crime is motivated by the need for more money to support a growing habit. At one time it was thought only the use of hard drugs (such as heroin, cocaine, pills) led to crime but supporting a marijuana habit can also be expensive.

Others seem to commit crime or get involved in juvenile troubles due to the influence of marijuana's high. Dean, a young teenage pot smoker, said: "Pot gave me a bad reputation. People started calling me a pothead and a thief. Sometimes pot gave me strength, and I would feel like fighting. I would fight a lot of times. Normally, I would not fight but pot made me feel macho. I'd go around jitterbugging, acting real bad .... I was walking down the street one day—under the influence of pot—and a cop across the street kept looking at me. I said, 'What are you looking at?' and he came across the street over to me and said, 'I'm looking at you now.' When he came right up to me and touched me, I kinda pushed him away. Then he started tangling me. He cuffed me; then he started choking me, beating me, and stuff like that. I was still under the influence [of marijuana] so I didn't feel it. They were holding my feet. I was still cuffed but I tried to bite him and do all kinds of things to him .... Pot gives me false courage. It makes you think you're tougher than you really are. Some people could handle it and some couldn't. I was the type that couldn't.

"So were some of my friends. One friend I remember smoked—maybe about an ounce and a half. He was really, really high. He killed somebody—just over fifty cents or something like that. He stabbed him in the heart. He's in jail now—he's a minor too. He was crazy but pot made him crazier .... I also know these guys who went into an old lady's apartment and sexually assaulted her. They were stoned. The fellow who was arrested for it was seventeen at the time. He's in prison now."

We do know there is a correlation between the use of alcohol and the committing of crime. Of the reported crimes, 50 percent are alcohol related. There are no studies available yet to show how much relationship there is between pot smoking and crime *but* if marijuana use follows a similar pattern to alcohol, then marijuana can directly or indirectly be a cause for criminal activities.

Dr. Bloomquist writes in *Marijuana: The Second Trip* that some of the reasons it is believed marijuana may stimulate criminal activity are:

1. It may be used by certain criminals to fortify their courage prior to committing crimes.

2. Chronic use of cannabis (usually hashish) may produce general mental derangement and demoralization leading to criminal activity.
3. Pot use may cause marginally adjusted persons to lower their inhibitions and behave in an aggressive, antisocial manner.
4. Cannabis may cause panic, confusion, or anger in otherwise normal persons who react adversely and then behave criminally as a consequence of their mental disorder.

The New "High" Class?

With all the data now available on the emotional, social, and psychological effects of marijuana's use, yet there is a grass-roots movement of young adults bent on perpetuating the idea that marijuana smokers are truly the "high class" of our society and that marijuana is a mild, pleasurable drug. I am alarmed when I read, for example, in the drug-culture magazine *Hilife* the following editorial:

> The fact of American society is changing. The generation that came of age during the '60s has produced a new culture, a pot culture that cuts across all class lines and, as a result, has had a great impact on the traditional leisure class in America.... I call this group the new high class, because leisure drugs have played such an important part in bringing together so many diverse segments of the population.
>
> We, the new high class, are held together by more than an interest in good dope. We have a sense of adventure. We're curious about the future and the newest trends. We believe in the equality of women. We like dope, sex, having a good time— and want our pleasures now. Today... we are the leisure class, an influential minority in America. Tomorrow, we will be the democratic majority.
>
> The new high class will be supporting efforts to abolish equally outdated federal and international laws that inhibit or prohibit the use of leisure drugs. In fact, sooner than most of us expect, leisure drugs will be designed by ethical pharmaceutical companies to increase our enjoyment of art, education, sports, sex, and other useful and entertaining pursuits.

Legalization—Then What?

I shudder to think what future generations may have to face if today's marijuana crusaders get their way. If marijuana is legalized—what next?

Underground scientists are now working on innovative drugs that may have the capacity of drastically altering or manipulating the senses in ways never yet experienced. Researchers have already developed several pills that amplify specific senses. The doper's magazine *Hilife,* in an article entitled "Pleasure Drugs in the Year 2000" stated: "... Pills can produce such precise functions as enhancing visual color sense or sensationalizing auditory power, without intoxicating or inducing hallucinations in the user."

Other drugs that some day could be peddled at the local drugstore are:

Mescaline—which eliminates fatigue and boosts motivation

Doet—which can focus the brain on specific thought patterns, which in effect can focus attention on previously unnoticed aspects of a situation

Coco chewing gum—to provide a quick stimulant that lasts for a short span of time. It would have the same effect as a pill but lasts only thirty minutes or so

We can also look for production of a more potent grass, such as hashish. What is not said behind the debate to decriminalize or legalize marijuana is the fact that many smokers will not be satisfied with low-grade, government-approved grass. This is evident by the increased amount of "good grass"—hashish and other stronger varieties of cannabis the police are confiscating. It is this higher-grade stuff that has potential for causing much more severe physical degradation and psychiatric disorders. Experts believe that adequately high doses of the active principles of marijuana can induce a psychotic reaction in almost anyone.

It is evident from all of this that marijuana is *not* the innocent, mild, recreational drug that its proponents would like to lead us to believe. When all the above data, comments, and interviews with pot smokers are taken into consideration, they reveal that the users know only one side of the story of marijuana's effects. As we will see in the next chapter, many young people are truly confused about the scientific surveys on its harmfulness. Many kids get their information about marijuana only from their pot-smoking friends or from such magazines as *High Times*, which states: "Reefers are good for everyone, regardless of age." Yet the magazine contains no information whatsoever on its hazards.

That marijuana is a "mild, pleasurable drug no worse than alcohol" is a bill of goods being perpetuated on not only our American youth but even on a nonsmoking adult population. Marijuana's harmlessness is a hoax and a falsehood. It is a trap that has the potential of harming perhaps millions of youth. *Changing Times* (March 1979) writes: "This trend towards use by children has caused second thoughts among some experts who in the past had not been unalterably opposed to the occasional recreational use of the drug by adults."

I do not want to overstate its possible damage to the bodies, minds, and characters of its users—but someone must set the record straight. It is true that previous generations used too many scare tactics to get kids off dope—especially marijuana. But this generation of users is just as guilty, in my estimation, with its casual "there's nothing to be concerned about" attitude. There is, right now, enough scientific and medical evidence piled up to blow the lid off all present arguments that have given rise to the decriminalization movement.

5
The Medical Case Against Marijuana

"What's the big scare about smoking marijuana?" said one user. "Pot never hurt anyone."

"It's no worse than alcohol," says another.

"A mild, pleasurable stimulant," says yet another.

For the past two decades, since the spread of marijuana use among young adults, teenagers, and young students—the question of marijuana's harmfulness versus harmlessness has been widely debated. As a result, the kids, both smokers and nonsmokers, are confused. Society has been sending mixed signals to our youth. On one hand, lawmakers have decriminalized marijuana-usage penalties, but on the other hand, many experts claim it is harmful and must be strictly controlled.

The jury has been out for too long now debating this question. It's time to examine the evidence and announce a verdict on marijuana.

Past Studies

Past conclusions on the weed's harmlessness were based on inconclusive studies of its effect, plus the fact that the number of users was significantly smaller than the present, and the strength of marijuana itself was much lower. This gave rise to promarijuana proponents such as NORML (National Organization for the Reform of Marijuana Laws) to call for its decriminalization and even legalization.

Even a National Commission on Marijuana and Drug Abuse (called the Shafer Commission) in 1972 prepared for the president and Congress a study called *Marijuana: A Signal of Misunderstanding.* The Shafer Commission unanimously recommended "that possession of a small quantity of marijuana for personal use should not be a crime."

Yet the Commission did not settle the question of marijuana's real danger. It only made the conclusion that the laws regarding it were too harsh.

Other authorities during the seventies presented a mild conclusion on marijuana including NIDA Director Robert L. DuPont, who was quoted in *Marijuana—The Facts,* a pamphlet distributed by the champion of marijuana, NORML. It stated: "... there is no question that alcohol and tobacco are causing us more health problems than marijuana does."

The Shafer Commission further concluded:

> From what is now known about the effects of marijuana, its use at the present level does not constitute a major threat to public health.
>
> Although a number of studies have been performed, at present no reliable evidence exists indicating that marijuana causes genetic defects in man.

For years NORML and millions of proponents of marijuana used such findings to enhance the liberal pot position. The result was that laws were changed, the attitude toward the smoker was softened, and the number of users skyrocketed. Until the late seventies and early eighties, the promarijuana findings went unchallenged and were accepted as true statements by many government officials. *Now that has all changed.* No reasonable person today believes marijuana causes less of a health problem than alcohol or tobacco. Scientific and medical evidence which is now available reveals that our previous verdict pronouncing marijuana innocent and harmless, was, to say the least, premature. The American public—and the millions who are now living (as well as dead) proof—have been duped by the dopers.

New Evidence of Pot Dangers

There are now a number of researchers, scientific experts, psychiatrists, psychologists, doctors, drug counselors, and educators, plus a vast host of present and former pot smokers who testify to its dangers. Among these are a growing number of past proponents of marijuana who have *now* changed their minds about it as a result of recent developments in scientific research. One such is psychiatrist Dr. Harvey Powelson. He was quoted in 1967 as saying, "Marijuana is harmless. There is no evidence that it does anything except make people feel good. It has never made anyone into a criminal or narcotic addict. It should be legalized." He no longer holds to this theory.

Listen magazine asked him, "Why did you change your mind?" His answer:

> Well, I was at the University of California when I made that statement. As director of the student health service, I was seeing a lot of patients and supervising people who were seeing many more. In the course of the next two years, either directly or indirectly, I saw literally thousands of students.
>
> One patient, whom I knew quite well and worked with for a long time, took up marijuana and hashish, which is a more concentrated form of marijuana, during the time I was seeing him. It became clear to me and my wife, who also saw him, that there was something changing about his ability to think, to remember, to judge, to understand.
>
> The things happening to his brain were things we could expect from someone who was having brain damage from alcohol or a tumor or organic brain damage. But he was a young healthy man. Then we discovered that the sessions that were particularly bad had occurred when he said he had used hashish within the previous two or three days. We both began to notice this connection.
>
> Then I began to see the same connection in other patients. Since then, a lot of recent scientific evidence has supported and explained these observations.
>
> I think marijuana is the most dangerous drug we have to contend with....

Much of the argument, pro and con, over marijuana the past ten years has been based on erroneous information gleaned from inconclusive and often contradictory reports. Dr. Robert L. DuPont contends that "a lot of the rhetoric surrounding the studies was unnecessarily confusing because the scientists were so concerned that their studies were going to be used by people who were antimarijuana, antiyouth or whatever, so they would always, it seems to me, conduct the research and report their findings in such a way as to add to the confusion. Now there is a greater willingness by scientists to state what is quite obvious but to state it in a clear way. That is, that marijuana is a health hazard."

Parents therefore who oppose their children's use of marijuana have had too few facts based on irrefutable research at their disposal. The latest research, however, shows that marijuana is definitely a harmful and dangerous drug. There are 60,000 people under the age of 18 in this country who require some kind of treatment for marijuana each year. In one large city hospital, out of over 4,000 cases admitted in a year's period for drug abuse, marijuana constituted 1,887 of those cases.

The proponents of legalized marijuana over and over again use the argument that "pot is harmless." Where do they get their data? Mainly from a few studies that produce seemingly inconclusive results. The key words here are *seemingly* and *inconclusive*.

The La Guardia Report

For example, one of the studies that the propot lobby points to is the La Guardia Report. Mayor La Guardia of New York City set up a committee in 1939—made up of twenty-eight doctors, pharmacologists, psychiatrists, and sociologists—to investigate the effects of marijuana in the United States. The outcome was a study that stated, among other things, that: "Marijuana does not change the basic personality structure of the individual. It lessens inhibitions, and this brings out what is latent in his thoughts and emotions, but it does not make responses which would otherwise be totally alien to him." It also stated that no mental or physical deterioration resulted from prolonged use.

The La Guardia Report has had widespread publicity. Is it accurate? Does it, as the proponents of marijuana argue, justify a change in the laws to make marijuana available to any and all who desire it?

Inconclusive Studies

There are several problems in basing a more liberal attitude toward marijuana on the La Guardia Report or other similar past studies, such as the Shafer Commission quoted previously. Such studies are inconclusive for several reasons:

1. **The strength of marijuana has drastically changed.** Dr. Robert DuPont, in an article in *Listen* magazine (March 1982) stated: "Most people developed their opinions on marijuana years ago, but today we face—*a whole new ball game.*"

The former director of NIDA, who made a 180 degree turnaround in his feelings about marijuana stated:

> The potency of the drug has changed. In the early '70's, we were talking about a drug that had a .2, .3 or .4 of a percent tetrahydrocannabinol (THC). I remember that during the early studies we did in the mid '70's, we were criticized for using a drug that had a potency of 2 percent THC. The criticism was that we were overdosing people on this drug, that it was irresponsible for us to be doing tests like that.
>
> Of course, all that's changed now. The typical marijuana used today in the United States contains four or five percent THC. So we've seen the potency increase over the last five or six years, somewhere between ten and twenty times, depending on what base line is used.
>
> That makes it a different drug and I think the scene we have now is totally new. The tragedy is that today's attitudes have not kept pace.

2. **The age of present users is much younger.** Past studies centered on long-term users, such as musicians, artists, poets, and other creative persons who use marijuana under a more controlled lifestyle. Today, while the substance in marijuana joints is more potent, the age of the user is much younger. The combination of these two factors is producing much different results and effects in the user.

Dr. DuPont, in the same article quoted above, said: "Part of the conflicting data from ten years ago had to do with the fact that we were talking about low-potency material being used by relatively healthy adults. Now we're talking about high-potency material being used by younger people who are more vulnerable to it."

3. **Today's pot smoker is living in a different society.** Also, today's smoker is often using marijuana for different and additional reasons than previously used. The effects of marijuana have a lot to do with the social environment and physical constitution of the user at the time or place of smoking.

Marijuana seems to be a "mood-extender." If one is happy when smoking, it can make him feel temporarily happier, or at least the illusion of happiness. However if the user's mood is down, pot will take him further down.

These factors, combined with the fact that society has gotten much more complex, with teenagers having difficulty developing a healthy self-image and direction in life, create circumstances in which pot is used more as a cop-out than a pleasure stimulant.

4. **Marijuana is much more available and the quality of it much more potent.** Kids are smoking pot more and enjoying it less—thus opening the door to more dangerous and potent drugs. Past studies surveyed users who were occasional, part-time, and recreational users. Today's smokers are using pot in the same manner as the drinker uses alcohol. It is inevitable, then, that the physical and psychological effects on the user are going to be different from those in the past.

"I think it's [evidence about what marijuana does] conclusive enough for me to take a firm position. Most of the jury is in on marijuana. I think the only additional thing we'll find out in the future is that it's more harmful than we now know. We already know it's harmful enough, that responsible people in the drug-abuse field will not recommend it for general consumption." (Forrest S. Tennant, M.D., Executive Director of Community Health Projects Inc., West Covina, California; quoted in August 1981 *Listen* magazine.)

Because so many people have been smoking pot over an extended period of time, there is now a wider sampling of abuses that doctors, medical researchers, and drug-abuse counselors have recorded as case histories from which they can draw some conclusions. Some sixty thousand cases per year need medical or psychological treatment for marijuana. These supply hard data as to whether the drug is as harmless as past conclusions and studies have shown.

The Medical Case Against Marijuana

Arguments That Pot Is Harmless

The proponents of legalized marijuana over and over again use the argument that "pot is harmless." They base this on two major arguments. First is the high number of persons, of all ages and classes, who smoke it socially and recreationally. "If so many are smoking it, it must be okay!" they reason. This is the "everybody's doing it" theory! How can so many be wrong?

Adding further fuel to their fire have been past studies already discussed. Until recently, the statements from earlier reports went virtually unchallenged and were accepted as true by many government officials. Now that all is changing.

Peggy Mann, in a *Reader's Digest* article entitled "Marijuana Alert II" states:

> All during this decade, evidence has been accumulating that smoking marijuana may be seriously injurious to health. In the past few years, striking new studies have further darkened the picture, demonstrating measurable harm to diverse body organs—above all, to the brain and reproductive functions. Today, the specter of a damaged human stock haunts scientific researchers and clinicians alike.

Set the Record Straight

What present-day studies reveal is that *pot is not harmless*. Most physicians involved in treating addicted patients agree that marijuana is a dangerous drug. New medical evidence is coming to the surface. The evidence is shocking and refutes the findings of past studies. Peggy Mann also states:

> Scientists from around the world are sending warning signals to the millions who smoke marijuana: Mounting evidence indicates that pot smokers may be unwittingly damaging their brains and decreasing their chances of conceiving and producing completely healthy offspring.

Hardin and Helen Jones declared in their book *Sensual Drugs:*

Marijuana is the most controversial of the sensual drugs. Because short-term use seemed to have little adverse effect and because, until quite recently, little was known about how the drug affected body chemistry, it was assumed that marijuana was like other well-tolerated drugs and medication. It seemed less harmful than other sensual drugs and incidents of lethal overdose were rare. The fact that it was referred to as a "mild" hallucinogen reinforced the idea that it was harmless.

The truth is that in the 1960's, when marijuana first became popular, the public was unaware of the consequences of its use. The fad was new, and users had not yet experienced the long-term effects. "Authorities" appeared on every side, each contradicting the others. Alarmists exaggerated the negative evidence; optimists preached the safety and benefits of marijuana use. . . . The facts, however, now rest on a firm scientific base; we now know some of the chemistry of the cannabis drugs and something of how they affect the body organs and cell functions.

The fact is no scientific evidence has been found to prove that marijuana is safe; we have only the personal testimonies of short-term users. [Italics, author's use.]

It is time, therefore, to set the medical and scientific record straight. Every parent, teenager (whether smoker or nonsmoker), teacher, clergyman, mental-health person—and others responsible for shaping the attitudes and opinions of the younger generation—must get this information out. It is time to counterbalance the carefully orchestrated public-relations campaign by the highly financed and powerful propot lobbyists and other proponents who would lead millions of kids to believe marijuana will not harm them.

I agree with David Toma when he says:

When it comes to mental health care, this nation is not in good hands. When it comes to mental illness that was caused by marijuana, almost all the professionals are inept at best, and in many cases, an absolute danger to their patients. Not many of them have done their homework where pot is concerned. Or if they have, they reject the research. Or they smoke pot

The Medical Case Against Marijuana

themselves. Or they just don't give a damn. Whatever the reason, a patient has to search hard and long to find someone in the mental health field who knows what is going on.

Consider what is now known about marijuana's effects on its users.

Effect on the Brain

One of the most tragic revelations from studying marijuana's effect on long-term users is what is called the "cumulative effect." That is, marijuana stays in the body for a long period of time. Dr. Powelson, in the previously quoted *Listen* interview, stated:

> It stays in the brain and it keeps operating long after people are high. This time element is anywhere from six weeks to six months. Biochemically, using tracers has proven that only half of the marijuana leaves your body in a week.
>
> Marijuana is soluble in oil and fat and totally insoluble in water. The ratio is 600 to 1, so that once it gets inside the cell, it can't get back into the bloodstream the way other drugs do. If you drink alcohol, it is soluble in water and also in the bloodstream. As fast as you drink it, it goes into the bloodstream and continues to circulate, and then it is burned and leaves the body.
>
> Marijuana just stays there. When marijuana users get high, it usually takes them two or three times, because they have to build up a certain amount in their brain. Once they get high, they take another joint and get a little higher, then the high drops off and they think they are sober again. But the marijuana is still active. When three days later they take another joint, then they get high again. But they are suffering the effects of marijuana all that time.
>
> It could be called a cumulative effect, but what I am really talking about is the fact that marijuana stays active in the brain long after the user feels high. It is very deceptive. Since it doesn't lead to staggering or leave a smell on your breath, nobody else can tell that you are high and you don't know

that you are high or whether you are stoned. Your brain isn't functioning right. And this can be proved. You can give a person mental tests before he takes a joint and then you can show that he can't do the same test as well for as long as 72 hours after the equivalent of 1 to 3 joints. It depends on the concentration.

If you ask somebody to take 100 minus 7 back to zero, he has to do two things at once. He has to remember what he is doing and he has to keep track of the last number. It is not very complicated but it is the kind of memory function that marijuana interferes with. Marijuana users tell that it focuses their attention. What that means is that they can't do two things at once. This particular memory test makes men do two things at once. If you time them on that test, it takes about 1½ minutes. Then they smoke three joints. A day later, it will still take them 1½ minutes to do the same test.

In real life, it is much more complicated. One of my patients was an airplane mechanic who worked on airplanes going from Alaska to Japan. He was staying stoned all the time. His supervisor didn't know it; nobody on the job knew it. He didn't care whether the instruments checked out or not. All he was interested in was staying stoned on the job. He wasn't thinking about anything but how good he felt. Yet pilots and passengers were depending on that man.

Right now some pilots in the mid-West are trying to get the Federal Aviation Agency interested in the fact that there are pilots and navigators and instrument testers who are stoned. Many people in this country—literally millions—are using marijuana and are stoned. And there may be people you and I are depending on to fly an airplane or drive a bus or perform our surgery or drive on the highway.

Some interesting experiments have been undertaken by Dr. Robert G. Heath, professor and chairman, Department of Psychiatry and Neurology, Tulane University of Medicine, New Orleans, Louisiana, in which extensive studies were done on the brains of monkeys exposed to marijuana. The studies found that the animals, after smoking marijuana heavily, showed lasting changes in brain function. The changes were reflected in recordings from electrodes implanted into deep structures in the brain. Furthermore, the recorded changes continued to persist up until four months after they had stopped smoking. When Dr. Heath was asked—in an interview published by *Listen* magazine, if he could draw any conclusions and give advice based on the hard facts of his study, he stated:

> Oh, yes. I think any agent that would affect a monkey would also affect a human. In view of this objective, scientific data, I would say that one would be unwise to expose himself to marijuana. It looks like a very damaging agent.
>
> We have seen these things go on in cycles. College kids used to take amphetamines to stay awake to study. This went on for a couple of decades until people began to realize how devastating "speed" was in terms of producing irreversible damage and creating behavioral problems. We are going to see the same thing happening with marijuana.

It is estimated that marijuana contains upwards of three hundred chemicals, sixty of which are found in no other plant. The principal psychoactive ingredient in marijuana, as mentioned before, is known as tetrahydrocannabinol or delta-9 THC. Doctors and researchers tell us that a few exposures to THC will not adversely affect the user, but it is the long-term accumulation of THC in the body that may damage body cells. No one really knows how long marijuana stays in the body. As much as 10 percent can remain as long as a week. Some studies have shown that, after 48 hours, more than half of the chemical breakdown products of marijuana were still in the body. Dr. Hardin B. Jones believes:

> A week after a person smokes marijuana, 30 percent is still in the body in the active form. There is no other drug or medication that I know of that lingers in the body so long. Of the portion that remains, the body retains 70 percent of that longer than the second week. It gets rid of only 10 percent a month after that, so the burden stays in the body for a long time, and as a person uses more and more, it accumulates.

It may be that the heavy pot smoker is never free of some of the effects of both THC and other ingredients in pot.

More recent studies on the effects of marijuana on teenagers found diffuse brain impairment. The symptoms of this are an inability to concentrate, loss of memory, and other learning disabilities, such as an inability to even write properly.

Dr. Heath, speaking at the International Symposium on Marijuana in Reims, France, in 1978 stated: "Clinical observations indicate that people might drink for years before serious brain damage occurs. But it would seem from the monkey studies that you have to use marijuana for only a relatively short time in moderate to heavy use before evidence of brain damage begins to develop."

Effect on Sex and the Reproductive Organs

Researchers have found that of all the adverse effects of marijuana, its damage and impairment of the brain and its harm to the reproductive system pose the greatest threat. Pot has an affinity for the brain and the sex organs. This is because the human brain has a large amount of fat, and marijuana, which remains in the body, is attracted to that fat. The testes and ovaries also have high fat contents.

What does marijuana buildup in these organs do?

Studies have shown that 44 percent of the THC females (laboratory-tested female monkeys) who had been given the human equivalent of one to three reefers a day, did not produce healthy, living offspring. The mothers lost their babies during pregnancy by abortion or stillbirth or by infant death soon after birth. (In comparison, the control group of undrugged monkey mothers had a 12 percent birth loss.) Other studies, on human females who smoked pot one to three times daily for at least six months prior to the studies, found that 38.3 percent of the women who smoked pot had defective menstrual cycles, compared to 12.5 percent in a control group of nonsmokers. Dr. Hardin Jones believes that "genetic damage is a very real risk." In a September 1977 *Listen* magazine article he stated:

> Marijuana is the most threatening substance known. No other environmental hazard is as likely to influence the health of those yet to be born. Persons smoking marijuana should pause and reflect on their responsibility for the health of their future children.

The Medical Case Against Marijuana

At the California Primate Research Center of the University of California at Davis, rhesus monkeys, whose reproductive systems closely resemble those of human females, were given raisin cookies spiked with milligram amounts of THC—the monkey equivalent of a human smoking one to two joints. The monkeys received this dose every day for three years.

Says Dr. Ethel Sassenrath, who conducted the study: "The THC-exposed babies that survived have acted differently from the others. They didn't seem to have normal 'breaks' on behavior. They showed defects in attention. This kind of subtle behavioral difference is characteristic of marginal brain damage in early development."

One of the most startling findings to come out of the International Symposium on Marijuana held in Reims, France, July 22 and 23, 1978, was the report a scientist at the conference gave on marijuana's effect on the male sperm. Scientists stated that there was a below-normal sperm count in both animals and humans exposed to marijuana, as well as marked increase in sperm abnormality. "Banana-shaped heads, formless heads, and broken hooks" were produced in the sperm by marijuana.

The message must be spread far and wide, to both the habitual and the occasional marijuana smoker. He or she may be playing genetic roulette.

Dr. Robert Peterson, of the National Institute on Drug Abuse states: "Despite thousands of years of alcohol consumption, not until recently did doctors discover that not very large quantities of alcohol can cause the fetal-alcohol syndrome, which results in abnormal babies. Therefore, pregnant marijuana smokers would be wise to heed the present warning signals before all the definite findings are in."

Effect on the Lungs

It is utterly foolish for anyone, be it the smokers or high-ranking government officials, to think that—in the words of the 1972 Shafer Commission report to Congress and the president—marijuana "use at the present level does not constitute a major threat to public health." This is especially true when there is so much medical evidence linking tobacco smoking with lung cancer and other diseases.

Marijuana is classified as a drug—tobacco is not. To believe tobacco is dangerous to one's health and marijuana is not is to be either naïve or ignorant.

Marijuana has far more tar in a stick than does a cigarette. The cancer-producing elements in tobacco are carcinogens. Marijuana has more of these agents in it than tobacco, and it stays in the lungs longer and gets down deeper in the bronchial tubes. Studies have shown that those who smoke marijuana for an extended period may develop chronic bronchitis and emphysema. Tobacco smokers have to puff for ten to twenty years before lung diseases appear; among hashish smokers, it can take as little as six to fifteen months. This is because, as mentioned previously, *one marijuana joint is the same as smoking one pack of cigarettes.* As a result, the user's lungs are blacker, due to the fact that the marijuana must be inhaled deeper and held in the lungs longer. *Sensual Drugs* states: "Autopsy examination of the lungs of heavy marijuana smokers show extreme breakdown in lung structure."

Studies have also shown that extended marijuana use produces a marked reduction in white-cell response, the body's prime defense against infection. THC seems to reduce the lung's capacity to kill bacteria. Thus marijuana smokers are more susceptible to colds, flu, and other normal germ infections.

Principal Dangers of Pot

Hardin and Helen Jones, in their book *Sensual Drugs,* list eight principal dangers of marijuana use. They are:

1. Unlike the other sensual drugs, marijuana's effects are usually not experienced the first few times a user takes it. Then, for a time, a very small dose produces an effect which leads the user to believe that marijuana is indeed harmless.

2. Because of the mildness of early withdrawal symptoms (as compared with those from other sensual drugs), the user thinks he is taking a mild drug and can easily withdraw any time he chooses.

3. Psychological conditioning to marijuana, in comparison with the apparent lack of chemical dependence, is strong.

The Medical Case Against Marijuana

The user is dependent on marijuana before he realizes it; a few regular or heavy users can stop without great effort.

4. The toxic substances in marijuana accumulate in the brain and the body tissues and will leave slowly. Most users do not know that most cumulative, noxious substances have long-range effects that are not evident from short-term use. Even mild use of marijuana (regular social use, for example) produces some long-lasting effects.

5. Tolerance to marijuana builds up so rapidly that most regular users need to progress to stronger or larger doses or to use the drug more frequently to feel the effects. What originally was a pleasant experience, in time is repeated only to avoid feeling bad. The majority of marijuana users do not stay with the occasional smoking of a mild marijuana cigarette.

6. The mechanisms in the brain that the user needs to evaluate his situation are disturbed by marijuana. The user, even when he is severely affected, cannot understand his problem.

7. For various reasons, many marijuana users tend to become smokers of tobacco, to use alcohol excessively and go on to use stronger drugs. The effect from a combination of drugs is compounded, not simply the sum of the effects of each.

8. Marijuana use has spread in epidemic proportions among the young, who have the most to lose from it. Marijuana can retard emotional development at a critical time in the maturing process. The adolescent is especially vulnerable, as he is developing new habits and ideas and integrating his personality into his surroundings. Sensual drugs alter body functions normally controlled by hormones. Now we know that hormone production is disturbed by marijuana. Sex hormones, delicately balanced in the adult, are in a state of flux in the adolescent.

The Joneses, in introducing the above material, stated: "We should look upon marijuana as the most potentially dangerous of the sensual drugs. We know now that its effects are deleterious but insidious and subtle. Even so, the full extent of its harmfulness is probably yet to be learned."

When the latest findings are looked at objectively, there can be no other conclusion than that of the former director of NIDA, Dr. Robert L. DuPont, who made the following statement in *Listen* magazine:

> I get a very sick feeling in the pit of my stomach when I hear talk about marijuana being safe. Marijuana is a very powerful agent which is affecting the body in very many ways. What the full range of these consequences is going to prove to be, one can only guess at this point. But from what we already know, I have no doubt that they are going to be horrendous.

This comment is especially significant since it was Dr. DuPont whom I quoted earlier as saying, "There is no question that alcohol and tobacco are causing more health problems than marijuana does."

Dr. DuPont told NBC news commentator Edwin R. Newman that he had changed his mind about marijuana, in that he now felt badly that he had contributed to the idea that marijuana was not dangerous.

Later Dr. DuPont also made this statement: "In all of history, no young people have ever before used marijuana regularly on a mass scale. Therefore our youngsters are, in effect, making themselves guinea pigs in a tragic national experiment. Thus far, our research clearly suggests that we will see horrendous results."

On July 24, 1981, the American Medical Association (AMA) made the following statements in a press release:

> There is now no doubt at all that marijuana is a dangerous drug, with great potential for serious harm to young users.... Marijuana is by no means the harmless instrument that many believe it to be....
>
> Target organ for marijuana is the brain. Structural changes occur in the brain with marijuana use, as well as changes in the pattern of brain waves. Acute marijuana intoxication impairs learning, memory, thinking, comprehension and general

The Medical Case Against Marijuana

intellectual performance. Even at moderate levels of social use, driving skills are impaired. . . .

Chronic use of marijuana may be associated with disruption of the menstrual cycle and at least temporary infertility. Miscarriage is more common among users. Among lab animals, sperm abnormalities have been noted along with damage to the male reproductive organs. Many physicians experienced in treating drug abusers believe that regular marijuana use may seriously interfere with psychological functioning, personality development and emotional growth and learning, especially in childhood and adolescence. The psychological damage may be permanent. Large doses of THC can induce hallucinations, delusions, paranoid feelings. Thinking becomes confused and disorientated. The initial euphoria may give way to anxiety reaching panic proportions.

Even moderate use is associated with school dropout, psychosis, panic states and adolescent behavior disorders. . . .

The American Medical Association is clearly on record as opposing legalization of marijuana for recreational use.

The time has come, therefore, for Congress, the police, local authorities, our schools and churches, parents, and the marijuana users themselves to discover what Dr. DuPont, the American Medical Association, and other experts have learned about the marijuana controversy—*and take a stand against its decriminalization and legalization.*

Presently many in society have committed themselves to a position on marijuana that, in light of the above evidence, must be reconsidered.

6
Decriminalization—Blessing or Curse?

A paperback novel entitled *Acapulco Gold* stated on its inside cover the scenario for the future of legalized pot:

To: MK & C
From: THE CLIENT
THE PRODUCT: MARIJUANA
The next President of the United States will legalize marijuana. We want to sell it to the American people.
THE MOTIVE: MILLIONS OF DOLLARS
The race is on. We're ready to grow and ship it. Can you sell marijuana like cigarettes? And can you do it first?

Read what happens in an advertising agency when it gets the jump on the promotion of the first legal marijuana cigarettes. And read what happens to the creative director handling the account, torn between the exciting campaign that would make history and his fears that, reports to the contrary, he is actually selling a dangerous drug.

The above is not science fiction. The prospects of Madison Avenue being able to launch a campaign to get your children and teenagers to turn on to pot may be just around the corner. If so, can other drugs, even more potent and dangerous, such as cocaine, heroin, and other twenty-first century drugs and highs be far behind?

Difference Between Decriminalization and Legalization

The major crusade organization for decriminalization and eventual legalization is NORML (National Organization for Reform of Marijuana Laws). Its small staff of full-time workers and a budget of over one-half million dollars a year "supports the removal of all

Decriminalization—Blessing or Curse?

criminal and civil penalties for the private possession of marijuana for personal use. The right of possession should include cultivation and transportation for personal use and the casual nonprofit transfers of small amounts of marijuana."

The above quote, taken from a pamphlet entitled "Official NORML Policy 1977," is the propot organization's stated policy and definition of the decriminalization of marijuana.

Decriminalization should not be confused with legalization. The latter would pave the way for commercialization of it, like liquor or tobacco. The goal of organizations like NORML and others who advocate decriminalization is, I believe, a first step to campaigning for its legalization. Once the more liberalized laws are in effect and the general public has gotten accustomed to the relaxed attitude, you can be sure the crusade to legalize will be pushed as hard as the present drive to decriminalize.

For now, the aim is to change the penalties for possession of small amounts of marijuana.

The marijuana laws did, and do yet in some cases, need changing. Some past and present laws treat marijuana use on the same level as heroin and other hard drugs. This was and is unfortunate and a mistake that should be corrected. Such severe laws have been used by the proponents of decriminalization as a justification for passing more lenient laws.

Changing Times reports:

> In Missouri, a college student is serving a seven-year sentence after he was convicted of selling $5 worth of marijuana to an undercover agent, and a twenty-year-old woman, convicted of splitting an ounce of the stuff with a date who turned out to be an undercover agent, was recently paroled for a five-year term in a prison farm there. An appeal to the courts by the young man with the help of NORML was denied and a letter-writing campaign coordinated by the organization failed to change the Governor's mind about the sentence. Now the constitutionality of the law is being challenged.

Such cases do point out the imbalance in drug sentences. But the pendulum is swinging now toward the side of tolerance. The Missouri student and other similar cases are used by organizations like NORML to gain sympathy for the decriminalization cause.

Laws in Various States

Eleven states—Alaska, California, Colorado, Maine, Minnesota, Mississippi, Nebraska, New York, North Carolina, Ohio, and Oregon have decriminalized marijuana. What this means is that possession of a small amount of marijuana, usually an ounce or less (enough for about fifty cigarettes), may result in a fine but no jail term or (depending upon circumstances) no criminal record. In Oregon, possession of up to an ounce is a civil offense on the same level as a traffic violation, carrying a maximum fine of $100. In Maine, the fine is up to $200; in Mississippi, $250.

Anyone caught with more than the maximum allowable amount may face the felony charge of possession with intent to sell. But in approximately forty other states, pot smoking is still risky business and the smoker faces stiff fines, a jail term and/or felony conviction. In Arizona, for example, a person convicted three times on a simple pot possession charge can be imprisoned for life. However, generally courts are deemed more lenient in sentencing pot offenders as they respond to the public's changing attitudes. Some judges are still handing down strong punishments, however.

What has been the effect of the reformed laws? Is decriminalization working?

In the states that still list possession of marijuana as a crime—39 to be exact—enforcement is generally lax and the pot smokers know it.

One of the most outspoken foes of the new laws is former Los Angeles police chief Ed Davis. "Decriminalization has increased the amount of marijuana, stimulated the use and trafficking," says Davis.

"We had been reducing the use of marijuana through good law enforcement. In 1971, the Los Angeles police department seized 16,392 pounds of marijuana. By 1975, we only picked up 4,990 pounds because we were discouraging its use. But in 1976, after decriminalization, we seized 17,916 pounds."

Davis did concede that the law charging marijuana smokers with

Decriminalization—Blessing or Curse?

a felony was too harsh. "Possession should be in the same class as intoxication, an arrestable misdemeanor," he stated.

A study prepared for the White House by a presidential panel set up in 1973 and revised by President Carter in 1977 (called the Strategy Council on Drug Abuse) stated:

> The past use of incarceration as a sanction against marijuana use has been irrationally applied, often with an extreme harsh punishment doing more harm to the individual than the drug itself.

But the report recommends that "the penalty should not be lifted altogether as this could be misconstrued to mean we condone marijuana use."

Effect of New Decriminalization Laws

There is no doubt that the new laws are increasing the use and abuse of marijuana. In 1962 only 4 percent of Americans aged eighteen to twenty-five had ever "used" marijuana, but by 1979, more than one-third (35 percent) reported "current use" (within the last month).

According to a most recent NIDA report (1981) two-thirds of one high-school class admitted to some drug abuse. Sylvia Porter, writing in a July 25, 1982 *Daily News* article stated that this is "higher than that of any other developed country in the Western world."

Of the 40 percent of American teenagers who are estimated to have smoked pot (Norman-Harris Report), "At least one out of ten young people leaving high school are daily users, and indications are that many continue their daily use into later life" (according to the University of Michigan Institute for Social Research, as reported in the *U.S. Journal of Drug and Alcohol Dependence,* October 1980, in an article entitled "Daily Pot Users Maintain Habit in Later Years").

I can rarely attend a major sporting event in the New York area or go anywhere where large numbers of youth are gathered without sniffing the distinct aroma of marijuana. Even walking down the street at times one can get a whiff of the smoke.

The decriminalization of marijuana has in effect said to young people, "Pot is okay." However, the lawmakers are talking out of both sides of their mouths. On one hand, they say it's okay to smoke it but on the other hand, they say it's not okay to sell it. By giving the okay to smoke it, they have opened the floodgates for the smugglers, traffickers, and the pushers. If it's okay to smoke it, in essence, they are saying it must be all right to sell it as well.

Forrest Tennant, quoted earlier, stated in an interview in the magazine *War on Drugs:*

> ... This time "decriminalization" means you let people grow it in their backyards. ... A drug is either legal or it's illegal. If it's legal, you put controls on it, you sell it in the right places to the right people; and if it's illegal, it's illegal and there ought to be a stiff penalty. It's as simple as that; make it one way or the other. ... As far as law enforcement, I think this movement towards doing away with the paraphernalia shops is very important. When you allow paraphernalia in stores and you have head shops, all that does is to tell people that drug use is okay, and we've got to have it where people are saying it, schools are saying it, churches and city councils are saying it; drug use is *not okay*. And be willing to take the criticism of the pro-drug people who say, "Drug use is great." You've got to have a backbone and say, "Drug use is not okay." It's as simple as that.

The Effects on Our Society

What have been and what will be the results of decriminalization on our society?

1. **Boys and girls will be smoking marijuana at younger ages.** Where states have lowered the drinking age, surveys show one result is that younger kids start drinking more. The twelve-, thirteen- and fourteen-year-olds who hang out with the older kids start drinking with their friends. The same pattern seems evident among teen pot smokers.

Congressional representative Lester Wolff (D NY), found this exactly to be the case. As Chairman of the House of Representatives' Select Committee on Narcotics Abuse and Control, he stated:

Decriminalization—Blessing or Curse?

"Evidence indicates pot smoking among eight- to twelve-year-olds is increasing."

What frightens me is the fact that the older, more stable youth may smoke pot for pure pleasure, then introduce some younger teen who has personal or family problems to the habit—and *he* starts using marijuana as a crutch. In my experience, drug abuse can turn a minor emotional disturbance in a teenager's life into a severe emotional problem. Older youth usually are better able, have matured enough, to face the realities of life. Young teens have not yet found alternate means of coping with problems, as adults often do. If smoking marijuana becomes the teenager's method of coping, he may never find a solution and become a habitual dropout or cop-out from society.

2. Where marijuana is pushed, there are often other drugs available. In the sixties, the argument against pot was that it always led to heroin. And that was true years ago in the ghetto. But when millions of middle-class youth started to smoke marijuana, the majority did not go on to hard stuff. The idea that marijuana led to hard-core addiction was abandoned, but it shouldn't have been—not entirely. My experience shows that for some types of youth, marijuana does become a lead-in drug to other more powerful and dangerous drugs. For example, cocaine is now the drug of choice among the more socially elite, while angel dust is the companion drug to marijuana on the streets.

I am convinced that anyone who starts using marijuana regularly and is given the right (I should say *wrong*) set of circumstances, will experiment with other, more potent drugs. This is the risk the pot smoker takes. The proponents of decriminalization have used this as an argument for controlling marijuana or even legalizing it. They say, "Take marijuana out of the hands of the illegal pusher and put it in the hands of government-controlled distributors, as is done with alcohol and tobacco. Thus we'll avoid having our kids buying pot from the street-corner pusher."

Were marijuana to be legalized, it would of necessity have to have its potency strictly controlled. Legalized pot would thus be in a mild form. Regular users would not get the desired effect. To be sure, the pusher would be there with better stuff. Decriminalization or legalization will not eliminate the black market in marijuana. And it's the illegal trafficker who has access to other dangerous drugs. To be sure, decriminalization or legalization will not put him out of business.

3. **Look for decriminalization to increase the number of addicts in our society.** My brother David and I wrote, in our book *The Untapped Generation,* a list of ten reasons *how and why young people experiment with and become dependent upon drugs.* It would be appropriate to list them at this point:

The Hows and Whys of Drug Dependency

The curious. Some young people are always curious about something that is mysterious, adventurous, dangerous, and illegal. But while curiosity is given as an excuse for having started a habit, it is often later found out that some character defect perpetuated the drug taking.

The weak willed. Some young people seek a simple, quick, magical solution to the problems of life and to their own character defects. Such young people need little urging to get them started and they find it difficult to put down the habit once it has been fixed. These include the severely inadequate, immature, and the lost and depressed.

The social addict or the social give-ins. These are young people who take drugs because it is the sociable thing to do. In their clique, everyone is doing it. Not to do so would mean to be left out. Taking drugs is a prerequisite for belonging to some groups.

The sense seekers. These are made up of the more artistic types who are seeking breakthroughs or a renewal of their creative power. They perpetually seek to spring free of their ordinary way of seeing or sensing the world around them.

Some users claim to have understood themselves better after taking the mind-expansion drugs. One boy said, "My mind opened up—I found out a lot of things about myself I didn't know—but I didn't like what I found. And I have no ability to do anything about the things I learned."

The escapers. These are young people seeking escape from boredom, responsibility, frustration, and anxiety. Many are affluent youths who have become bored with blessings. They don't know how to get high on life. They cannot accept responsibilities or the difficulties that make a young person grow. Life turns them *in*, not *on*.

The accidental drug user. This is a young person who has been turned on to drugs by a friend, relative, or some older person. The young person taking the drug did not really know what he was getting involved in and accidentally got hooked.

One fellow related, "My best friend gave me a marijuana joint. Although I knew it was dangerous, I trusted him and so I thought everything would be all right. I had a pleasant drug experience and so started smoking from time to time with him until I woke up one day and found myself hooked." Although the young man was not completely naïve to the drug scene, he nevertheless accidentally became involved because he trusted a friend.

The persuaded addict. Related to the social and the accidental user are those who have been persuaded to indulge. A husband persuades his wife; a boyfriend turns on his girl friend. The user may go along because of some misguided sense of love or in the case of some young women, because of some idea that if she were involved, she would be able to help her man with his drug problem.

The prescription addict. Some get involved in drug addiction through physical problems for which the doctor prescribed a certain drug. However, they find that while the drug alleviates their physical problem, it creates a worse one in that they develop a psychological dependence of which they are unaware. Prescription addicts are often people who started their drug use under extreme stress.

Stone heads. This is the type of young person who has found absolutely no meaning or value in life. He has come to the conclusion that anything is better than what he has experienced. He will take anything and everything, perhaps even a combination of drugs and alcohol.

The religious seekers. A growing number of young people use drugs as a religious sacrament. They seek personal insights or religious experiences. More frequently, they use psychedelic drugs (LSD and others). They are searching and believe that these drugs open up new levels of spiritual understanding.

Marijuana has the potential to introduce the entire drug world to each of these ten types of indulgers. To many, perhaps millions, marijuana and marijuana alone is the drug of choice. They smoke pot but do not indulge in other more dangerous drugs. *But there are a percentage of marijuana smokers who turn from being regular users to regular abusers and then go on deeper and deeper into the drug scene, eventually getting themselves hooked, either physically or psychologically, or both.* The more pot smokers, the more potential for a percentage going on to the real addictive drugs. It is this percentage, as small as it may be in proportion to the total number of pot smokers, yet numbering in the tens and hundreds of thousands, that strict marijuana laws are intended to protect. If we can ban a dangerous food additive that could cause cancer to a very small percentage of Americans, then by the same reasoning we must provide strict laws to control a substance that has the potential of destroying even a small percentage of our total youth.

4. **Increased death and injury on the nation's highways.** When the first talk about liberalized marijuana laws was advanced, I stated, "The potentially most dangerous result of widespread marijuana use is going to take place on the nation's highways. In addition, how would you like your doctor to be puffing on a joint before operating on you, or the pilot of your airplane or the taxi or bus driver?" Until recently, there has been almost a total unawareness of drivers who are intoxicated on pot. Most states have tests to establish alcohol intoxication, but there is as yet no effective test to detect drivers who are under the influence of marijuana.

According to an article in the May 1979 *Reader's Digest:*

> A growing number of stoned motorists are endangering lives on the highways.... Recent studies blow the warning whistle

on a little publicized but nonetheless frightening new menace to motorists; the pot smoker driving "high" on the highways. Persuasive evidence is mounting that such drivers often have a distorted sense of space and time, altered peripheral and central vision, impaired manipulative and coordinative skills.

Relaxed pot laws have given smokers the idea they can smoke their weed anytime and anyplace they want, similar to lighting up a cigarette. This is putting potentially dangerous maniacs behind the wheel of an automobile, adding to the already outrageous problem of the drunk driver. Richard L. Burton, former commissioner of Alaska's Department of Public Safety, quoted in the above *Reader's Digest* article, stated: "The alcohol problem on the highways will soon be only half as serious as marijuana and that's not because alcohol is going to get any better."

Hugh Alcott, project manager of the California Department of Corrections Special Narcotics, quoted by Peggy Mann in a September 1981 *Saturday Evening Post* article entitled "Death on the 'High-' Way" stated:

> A lot of people who had too much to drink and know their driving skill will be affected, smoke a joint "so they can drive better." They actually believe that marijuana acts as an antidote to the effects of alcohol. All that pot does, of course, is to make them *feel* they're driving better. In fact, their driving is far more impaired than if they'd used alcohol alone.

Surveys reported by the National Institute of Drug Abuse reveal that 60 to 80% of marijuana users questioned indicated that they sometimes drive while cannabis intoxicated.

How does marijuana affect driving?

Dr. Robert Moscowitz, as quoted in the *Saturday Evening Post* article (September 1981) by Peggy Mann, states: "The predominance of evidence indicates that marijuana impairs skills performance, perceptual process, attention and tracking behavior. All important components of driving and skills performance are thus clearly affected."

One young smoker confessed that marijuana affected his driving. "At times and under certain conditions, it was as though the oncoming cars had slowed down," when in fact they had not. He said, "The most scared I was ever in my life is when we left a party and I went with a friend on his motorcycle. He was stoned! He drove off the road and into a tree. I was not hurt bad—but my buddy was killed."

Effects of Marijuana on Drivers

The problem of time/speed distortion seems to be only one of the ways marijuana affects drivers. Researchers have discovered *marijuana intoxication* causes some of the following:

1. Peripheral vision narrowed or blocked out
2. Oncoming visual perception impaired
3. Reflex impairment: the inability to brake at normal reaction times or to react to other drivers
4. Impairment of night driving: night lights and glares are difficult to adjust to in the same manner as when not intoxicated
5. Coordination and control skills impaired: skills such as passing other cars, turning sharp curves, turning around or traffic merging, which under regular conditions are done out of natural habit, are all messed up when marijuana intoxicated

A few states, but only a few, have finally recognized the potential danger of accidents, injuries, and death that are resulting from this "high-"way driving and have passed laws to combat it. At present, there are no tests available to give drivers to detect quickly and simply if they are marijuana intoxicated. (However, a machine is being tested now which may soon change this.)

Of the eleven states that have decriminalized marijuana, only Alaska and Minnesota have enacted a special penalty for possession of pot in a vehicle.

A California Department of Justice study, in which 1,792 blood samples were taken from drivers arrested for traffic accidents or for driving under the influence of drugs, found 16 percent had sufficient THC in their blood to constitute marijuana intoxication. Only one-half of the drivers arrested had agreed to give a blood sample.

Some tests have shown that drivers under the influence of a large

Decriminalization—Blessing or Curse?

dose of marijuana show a decline of 42 percent in driving skills and the high-dose subjects had a 63 percent decline. Others studies show "a definite decrease in skills and performance five to six hours after taking a strong social dose of marijuana ... and lingering effects as long as twenty-four hours later."

The worst part about the marijuana-intoxicated driver is his ability to conceal it and his unawareness of how his ability is impaired. The drunk driver usually finds it difficult to hide his condition, especially if stopped by the police. *Reader's Digest* states: "This apparent ability to 'hide the high' gives most pot smokers confidence that they can drive stoned." Even NORML recognizes the danger of driving under the influence of marijuana and "strongly discourages the driving of automobiles or other vehicles while under the influence of marijuana or any other drug, and recognizes the legitimate public interest in prohibiting such conduct."

A 1981 AAA Foundation for Traffic Safety asked five thousand high-school students in one hundred schools their feelings about the danger of pot smoking and driving. More than half said marijuana had "harmful effects on driving, braking, and making decisions, reacting to emergency and obeying traffic signals." Sixty-seven percent said marijuana harms the ability to "stay in one lane"; and 71 percent said it "harmed the ability to pay attention."

5. Decriminalization of marijuana will result in economic loss to our nation. We already have two serious intoxicants draining the nation's economy—tobacco and alcohol. Nicotine is said to cost us 60,000 to 300,000 deaths per year and over $20 billion in economic loss.

Alcohol has produced nearly 10 million alcoholics. The financial, social, and human waste this has brought upon society is so pervasive there is hardly any area of our lives not affected by it. An estimated 100,000 persons yearly die from alcohol's effects, with an economic loss of $30 billion.

Are we ready to add another intoxicant—marijuana—to these two? P. Zeidenberg, in a report to a United States Senate hearing in 1974, stated:

> ... there is no question in my mind that legalization of marijuana will lead to a large population of chronic heavy marijuana users, numbering in the millions, just as prevails with

alcohol and tobacco. Both of these latter agents exact a terrifying toll in human life, suffering, and expense in this country annually. I think it is probable that heavy marijuana use in our country would create a third at-risk population, overlapping only in part with the two previous groups and further add to mortality, morbidity and public cost.

It is estimated that the dollar cost for the killing and injuring of people on the highways, as a direct result of drug abuse, is some *$20 billion* in wasteful, unproductive expenses, including $6.7 billion in medical, rehabilitation, and other direct outlays and $13.5 billion in lost productivity.

Many authorities are also concerned about the effects to the U.S. economy due to the burgeoning "underground economy." This is the billions of dollars each year measured in goods and services (including illegal drug sales) that is carried on "under the table." An April 19, 1982, *U.S. News & World Report* article stated:

> Economists gauge the underground economy's size in the hundreds of billions of dollars a year as measured in goods and services. That's a total that exceeds the entire gross national product of many countries. Subterranean dealings are estimated to equal 14 to 30% of the above-ground U.S. GNP of approximately $3.1 trillion dollars a year.... Also puffing up the undergound economy are illegal aliens, drug pushers, loan sharks and others who normally would not come forward and file [tax] returns in any case. The IRS says narcotic dealers alone evade up to $8 billion a year in taxes.

6. **International repercussions.** Some of our foreign allies do not understand why America is flirting with the legalization of marijuana. In countries like South Africa, Brazil, Turkey, and Greece, where cannabis has been used for centuries, they now have severe laws banning its use.

What has not gone unnoticed by modern leaders in North Africa is the devastating effect drugs, particularly hashish, had on the old Arab world.

Decriminalization—Blessing or Curse?

Historians believe they know one of the reasons the so-called Golden Age of the Arab world passed into history, when virtually all provinces of the Moslem world flourished, especially in North Africa. It was a direct result of the widespread use of the drug hashish. There was no evidence in the early centuries of Islam—including the Golden Age—of the drug being used among the population at large. But slowly social decadence and degeneration crept in. Among other factors was the widespread use of hash, which can be smoked, chewed, eaten in a confection or as a drug for its intoxicating effects. The use of this drug is believed to have been a major contributing factor taking its toll on the old Arab society—with devastating effect more than any disease epidemic or even a war could have had.

Even today, the use of drugs in certain countries such as Morocco, where *kif* is grown in large quantities as a major crop and is smoked by a high proportion of adult males and a significant number of females as well, keeps the society in a state of continual stagnation.

Egypt had such an epidemic of marijuana use during Nasser's rule. He spent a lot of money for an extensive study of marijuana. It was undertaken by an American-trained scientist and published in ten volumes in Arabic. It showed, in a very scientific way, that without question, marijuana affects people's ability to function.

The United States is a part of an international agreement with other nations to "limit exclusively to medical and scientific purposes the production, manufacture, export, import, distribution of, trade in, use and possession of drugs."

Many people in our Justice Department feel that if our marijuana laws are relaxed too far, our positions on harder drugs will be in jeopardy in terms of our agreements with other countries.

It is interesting to note, as has one Swedish authority:

> Demand for legalizing cannabis has been strongest in those countries which have had the shortest experience and the weakest form of the drug. In all the twenty-one countries my wife and I visited during a study of drug-abuse problems, and particularly in the countries where cannabis use is endemic, people were dismayed to hear of the attempts in the U.S. to

legalize marijuana. They felt that legalization would allow drug use to spread through the entire population ... and it is felt to be a factor in keeping the poor impoverished.

7. The drive to decriminalize is a calculated step by the proponents of marijuana to legalize it. At first the advocates of decriminalization claimed, in their testimony before state legislatures preparing to vote on decriminalization laws, that they did not favor legalization. Yet within weeks after such state laws were passed, these same people began making speeches calling for full-scale legalization.

Marijuana Lobbyists

The decriminalization people use their campaign as a front and a smoke screen to hide their legalization movement, because they know the public is not ready for the latter—yet.

In New York State, the marijuana lobbyists got behind a bill to legalize marijuana for medical purposes (it is said to aid the sight of those suffering from glaucoma and to relieve the side effects of chemotherapy in cancer patients). Again the purpose was to "get whatever we can," as one marijuana advocate stated.

An organization calling itself Committee for the Abolition of Marijuana Prohibition (CAMP) claimed to have pressed a nationwide voter-registration drive prior to the 1980 presidential election under the banner LEGALIZE MARIJUANA—REGISTER TO VOTE. A spokesman for the group stated: "We have to make politicians aware that those people who are out in the streets demonstrating are registering to vote." They felt former President Carter owed them a debt, in that many voted for him in 1976 because they thought he would push for the legalization of pot after that election.

In mid-1982 an independent Washington, D.C., organization, the National Academy of Science, caused quite a stir when its eighteen-person panel added further confusion to the question of whether marijuana laws should or should not be tougher. The Academy's Committee on Substance Abuse and Habitual Behavior turned in a report in its study of marijuana laws which found evidence of the drug's physical and emotional dangers to justify "serious national concern."

Decriminalization—Blessing or Curse?

However the committee's assignment was to look at the cost to government and society of enforcing the criminal laws against marijuana. They concluded they were too high. "Tough laws do not appear to deter marijuana use," said the committee.

Once again, this committee's study and conclusions is a case in point of trying to have both ways. They could not deny marijuana is a health danger—yet they try to argue that the possession or private use of marijuana could no longer be a crime.

Reaction to the committee's report was swift and harsh. Even the president of the National Academy of Sciences disavowed its recommendations. Given the public reaction, the Committee itself seemed to want to let their report fade into oblivion. NIDA director Dr. William Pollin was "not pleased" with the report. Pointing to recent surveys that indicate high-school seniors are turning away from pot, he said it would be "a terrible mistake and a public health tragedy [to do] anything that suggests a greater societal acceptance of the use of marijuana, particularly by young people."

Time magazine in its July 19, 1982, Law section stated in an article entitled "The Potshot That Backfired":

> ... The report may have ignored the temper of the times. Ten years ago, the public was moving towards the idea of lighter punishment for marijuana users. A 1972 study by the National Commission on Marijuana and Drug Abuse concluded that criminal sanctions were failing and counterproductive. Over the next six years, eleven states decriminalized pot possession for individual use* while many others decreased penalties or loosened up their enforcement. President Carter backed a softening of federal laws. But by the late '70s the mood began to swing back. With an estimated 60% of high-school seniors having tried pot and the drug making inroads at elementary schools, frightened parents dissuade legislators from further liberalization. In step with this sentiment,

---

*Citations and small fines have replaced arrests and incarceration in Alaska, California, Colorado, Maine, Minnesota, Mississippi, Nebraska, New York, North Carolina, Ohio and Oregon which in aggregate have one third of the U.S. population.

the Reagan administration's firm antidrug stand includes pot. Says Dr. Carlton Turner, the President's chief narcotic policy advisor: "There are 60,000 people under the age of 18 in this country who require some kind of treatment for marijuana each year."

If I can find any benefit in the results of decriminalization of marijuana, it has been the opportunity to weigh the full impact legalization would have on our nation's youth and the whole of society. The prospect of machine-packaged legal pot being sold over the counter is one of the most frightening prospects that faces this and future generations. It could have a devastating impact on our teenage and young-adult life-styles. I hope we've seen enough already to make us want to call a halt to the move to further decriminalize or legalize marijuana.

7
Parent Power

A most unusual phenomenon began to take place in our society as the decade of the 1980s dawned. A new revolutionary group has begun to flex its emotional muscles: I speak of *parents*. After several decades of a child-centered, youth-centered, me-centered society—giving rise to a "do your own thing" philosophy—parents have begun to wake up and exert their rightful place and power in the home, schools, community, and even in respect to government policies.

End of Permissive Society?

Nowhere is this parent power better seen than in public and parental attitudes toward drug abuse. The *U.S. News & World Report* in its June 28, 1982, issue stated in an article entitled "End of the Permissive Society?": "The era of 'let it all hang out' is giving way to a new, tougher approach to crime, drugs, many other social problems." The article refers to such parent power being demonstrated in actions such as:

1. Cracking down on drunk driving (responsible for half of last year's five thousand highway deaths).
2. More mandatory sentences for certain crimes and longer confinement for repeat offenders.
3. The forming of self-help programs by parent groups with out-of-control drug-abusing teenagers, using firmness and discipline to restore a more traditional family environment.

The article further states:

At the same time, a self-styled "citizens' war on drugs" is making an impact in almost every state, with new laws aimed at everything from drug smuggling to shops dealing in drug equipment.

This parent movement actually began in the late 1970s in Georgia and Florida. By the early 1980s, the "family action antidrug movement" had swept across the country with more than one thousand individual groups.

The magazine *Focus on Alcohol and Drug Abuse* comments on this family-action movement by saying that "it reflects just how deeply growing numbers of the nation's parents feel about the impact of marijuana on their children's lives.

"It's a movement that gives good indication it might succeed in holding back the drug tide where established drug-abuse program professionals at federal, state and local levels have previously failed."

These parent groups sprang up when they realized that despite all of the government funds being allotted to drug-prevention programs during the sixties and seventies, those programs had failed. They saw the drug pushers and promoters winning out, plus the passing of decriminalization laws with not so much as a word of resistance by the nonpot-smoking public. This gave rise not only to the high profits from drug sales, but those who were caught were going unpunished. In addition, the whole drug-related industry boomed. Drug paraphernalia stores called "head shops" and magazines like *Hitimes* popularized and glamorized drug use as socially acceptable—a new recreation of this era.

Finally some parents said *"Enough."* The result is that parent power has been unleashed.

One group, the National Federation for Drug Free Youth, was formed as an umbrella organization for over three hundred individual parent organizations representing groups from across the country. Their primary purpose is to inform and educate parents, adolescents, and children and others about the dangers of marijuana and other mind-altering drugs: they also promote and assist the formation of local parent groups throughout the United States. Their primary purpose or ultimate goal is to curtail the use of *all drugs among youth.* Their address: 1820 Franwell Ave., Room 16, Silver Springs, MD 20902.

CDU and "Responsible" Use

What upsets many of these parent groups and individual parents as well is the drive by some in society for "responsible drug use." This "if you can't quit drugs then try to live with them" philosophy is being put forth by organizations such as Conscious Drug Use (CDU). CDU was founded and is run by Tommy Rettig, who from 1954-1958 was the original star of TV's "Lassie." CDU tries to teach "responsible management" of drugs such as alcohol, tobacco, marijuana, and cocaine. Rettig has been arrested three times on drug-related charges, thus his personal motivation in trying to promote "responsible" drug use.

Tom Adams, head of NIDA's Supported Pyramid Prevention Project states: "To parents you cannot talk about the responsible use of an illegal drug by a child. By its very nature, such use is irresponsible."

Joining the antidrug campaign has been First Lady Nancy Reagan. Speaking to one of the antidrug parent federation groups, she advised them to get tough, even if it means "losing your child for a while." She labeled addiction "the most democratic illness there is," because it cuts across all racial and economic lines.

"I believe parents are the answer to it all," Mrs. Reagan told the White House visitors. "I think for a long time parents weren't involved. They shifted it to the schools or the police or the government. Anybody but themselves, because it took time, it took effort, it's not pleasant.

"Sometimes you run the risk of losing your child for a while. You have to be tough and you have to learn to say 'no.' You can't only say 'yes.'

"It's great to be your child's friend or pal," she said, "but sometimes you've got to be his parent."

Mrs. Reagan added, "Drug and alcohol abuse is one of the most serious problems our country faces." She quoted an old adage: "A woman is like a tea bag. You never know her strength until she's in hot water." She said this applies to men as well. "We're all in a lot of hot water.... There's a danger of losing our whole next generation."

Return of Parent Action

One group that refuses to sit back while kids abuse themselves with drugs is MADD—Mothers Against Drunk Drivers. Their efforts have been in obtaining mandatory sentences for drunk drivers. One of the founders, Cindy Lightner, says, "As it stands now, drunk-driving manslaughter is a socially acceptable form of homicide. That is why we are MADD."

This swing away from parental permissiveness into strictness is a healthy sign. It comes after several decades of an overemphasis of parental restraint and of parents being told and made to feel that they don't know what to do with their kids, so let the so-called experts tell them how to do it.

So they did! When the kids got into trouble, they blamed the schools for not preventing drug abuse. Massive drug education programs were then instituted. If a kid got caught smoking pot, the parents looked for outside help in self-help groups, psychiatrists, psychologists, and other so-called professionals. When the kids got busted for using dope, parents cried out for more police power.

Now parents realize they must first take matters into their own hands. Many are, and in addition are getting involved outside the home and in the schools and communities to wage antidrug campaigns. Also, they are adopting "spare the rod and spoil the child" philosophy within the home. Jean Westin tells in her book *The Coming Parent Revolution* "why parents must toss out the 'experts' and start believing in themselves again." She further states:

> In the 1980s, the priority for parents is to recreate a family ethos that will act as the fortress against outside disruptive forces. Although sociologists have long told us that the child-centered family is inward turning, I believe the opposite is true: Child-centered families turn *outside* to experts, children turn *outside* to peers. What we need is the family-centered family that turns inward to its values for strength.
>
> Parents of the parent revolution must offer this society the working model of family-centered family carrying forward the traditions of the past—not as a millstone but as a stepping-stone to a better, happier future for parents and children alike.

Toughlove

One group of parents has formed an organization called Toughlove, based on this philosophy. With strong support and publicity from Ann Landers, Toughlove is for familes who have out-of-control teenagers. Its primary goal is to restore parental authority through firmness and discipline. Even its logotype vividly demonstrates its objectives—a fist within a heart.

"You're the boss," says a Toughlove manual. "The sooner your youngsters understand this, the better."

Parents involved in this nonprofit self-help group say it helps them get rid of parental guilt feelings and provides information and inspiration in dealing with kids in the family who are not in trouble. Toughlove parents are encouraged to set specific penalties for drug-abuse offenders in the home, such as forbidding use of the family car, limiting phone calls, refusing to interfere when a child gets into trouble, or sending a repeatedly troublesome teenager to live elsewhere.

The Get High on Yourself Campaign

The move to fight back against drug abuse is not limited to parent groups. Individual efforts are worth noting. For example, Cathy Lee Crosby, founder and chairperson of the Get High on Yourself Campaign, says the nonprofit foundation was formed "to create an alliance with the private sector; it is an organized task force of corporations, individuals, groups, and kids. The foundation is not affiliated with any political party, religion, organization, or governmental body. The purpose is to get kids high on themselves by offering productive and positive alternatives to drug usage, both through a concentrated national media-awareness campaign and a continuing grass-roots effort, which will enable the kids to participate actively in the solution to the problem through specific Get High on Yourself programs." The organization's address: Box 67400, Los Angeles, CA 90067.

With Bob Evans, Cathy Lee Crosby coproduced a prime-time special for NBC in September 1981. The documentary involved a cast of personalities from the entertainment field, and kids. Its message was summed up in the theme song:

> You can be somebody with a plan
> of your own,
> You can say no and you won't be
> alone.
> You can make yourself get higher
> than you have ever known,
> By making up your own mind,
> doing things your own way,
> setting up your own style by being yourself.

Used by permission. "Being Yourself" words and music by Steve Karmen © 1981 Elsmere Music, Inc. All rights reserved.

A Concerned Chicago Cop

Another person who decided to make up his own mind, at the very risk of his life, was Chicago policeman James Watson.

In 1967 he became a Chicago cop. According to a *Time* magazine (July 26, 1982) article, "He made a great cop . . . as a decoy mugging victim, undercover narcotics, and organized-crime investigator. . . ." He was dedicated to his job and to his fellow policemen.

But the police scene changed. Watson became disturbed by the pot smoking and cocaine snorting of his fellow officers. At first, the drug use was confined to home and off-duty locations, but then the users got bolder and bolder—even selling it from squad-car windows. When he protested, the newer and younger officers told him this was the way it is with a modern-day cop.

Initially he turned away from such goings-on until, as reported in the *Time* article, "responding to a routine call, Watson radioed for another patrolman to join him. The officer never came. He was too high, too jazzed up on cocaine to do his duty."

Watson went to a former colleague in the Chicago Internal Affairs Division, ended up becoming an undercover agent for them, and was instrumental in helping to "bust" ten dope-using cops.

Time says: "Watson is not rejoicing. He and his wife and their children are now in a different city, living under an assumed name. His former buddies, he says, 'wouldn't mind killing me.'"

It is just such acts of heroism that it takes to make our youth today know that someone is serious about putting a stop to drug abuse. It is not uncommon to see and hear a drug bust *of* police *by* police. As shocking as this is, it was and is inevitable, given the permissiveness and tolerance toward drugs in our society. We need more James Watsons as well as others, to attack rather than retreat when drug abuse gets close to home.

The Vanishing Head Shops

Perhaps one of the greatest feats that the parent and family antidrug movement has been able to accomplish is in helping to change government legislatures' minds about drug laws. Particularly they have almost singlehandedly been instrumental in getting laws passed to shut down the head shops, which sell drug paraphernalia. Such shops have been, for these parents' groups, the focal point of their war against drug abuse.

The drug paraphernalia business is a $3 billion-a-year industry, complete with its own trade association.

The impetus for legislation against the paraphernalia industry came when the United States Drug Enforcement Administration (DEA) drafted a bill in 1979 which called for the banning of sales or possession of paraphernalia "associated with drug use." The antidrug groups had been the strongest lobbyists for such laws, and as a result, twenty-six states have adopted some version of the DEA drawn bill.

As soon as enacted, the bills began to be challenged in the courts and finally, an Illinois village ordinance reached the Supreme Court. The village of Hoffman Estates, Illinois, enacted an ordinance which provides for the licensing of premises on which "paraphernalia" is sold and ban sale of it to minors in the village. The high court upheld the village ordinance and rejected a challenge that regulation was unconstitutional on its face. In the same week, the court declined without comment to hear pre-enforcement challenge to two state paraphernalia laws.

Lee Dogoloff, Executive Director of the American Council on Marijuana states: "No longer is there the hopelessness and frustration about pot and other drugs that inhibited so many Americans before. The prevailing mood now is that the battle can be won."

What has happened since the passing of the paraphernalia laws? In Idaho, a shop owner faces nine years in jail and a $30,000 fine, having been busted under a DEA Model Act-type state law prohibiting "smoking accessories and novelties" in general.

In Georgia, head shops have recently been swept clean by narcotic agents.

Even the popular dopers' magazine *Hitimes* allegedly has been hurt by the antiparaphernalia laws because advertisers of paraphernalia items have backed off from placing their regular ads in that magazine. According to one report, magazine sales are being hurt by store owners who are putting up signs on their windows saying, "This store will not sell *Hitimes* magazine." The sign carries the emblem of the National Anti-Drug Coalition.

While all of the antidrug groups are important and their assistance in getting laws passed is good and necessary, in the final analysis, it is what *each parent* does in each individual home that ultimately makes a difference as to whether a child or a teenager turns to drugs.

8
How to Guard Kids Against Drugs

Drug prevention must begin in the cradle.

In *Fast Track to Nowhere* (which deals with the shocking facts about teenage drinking), I wrote:

> Drug and alcohol prevention is not so much a classroom program of education as it is a process of continual education in the home.... The two greatest factors in causing teenage drinking [the same can be said for marijuana] are peer pressure and parental influence. The best of homes and parents can do little to remove the child or teen from the pressures to drink they will face in school at extracurricular activities or among neighborhood youth. But children who have their physical, emotional, and spiritual needs met at home, have the best chance of not caving in or giving in to peer pressure when it comes to drinking, using drugs, sexual promiscuity, and other teenage "curiosities."

I believe there are a few important things parents can do to create a right atmosphere in the home and instill in their children the necessary character to help them face the inevitable outside influences (be it pot or whatever).

Home Prevention Remedies

I would like to list here the home remedies for drug prevention as adapted from chapter 8 of *Fast Track to Nowhere,* entitled "Prevention."

1. Properly communicate a value system when talking or teaching on the dangers or evils of drugs. This is the generation that asks,

"Why?" In answer to a question as to why they are using drugs, the answer "Why not?" may come back. They feel that "it's my body" and thus they have a right to get high. When parents flatly state "no drugs," they are going to have to give valid reasons why not and communicate them through not only words but by the example of their own life-styles. Studies have been conducted that show kids whose parents abuse alcohol, pills, and other medications are more likely to use marijuana and other drugs themselves.

Parents must create a good communication atmosphere with their kids to discuss marijuana on a factual level, not purely on an emotional level, such as, "I'd better not catch you smoking pot!" Parents must give their kids valid reasons why not when it comes to drug experimentation and drug abuse.

In a *Focus on Alcohol and Drug Issues* magazine article entitled "What You Can Do Within Your Own Family," the following helpful recommendations are made:

> You do not need to "rap" or talk street slang with your child. She or he needs to hear an adult point of view on drugs; s/he gets enough rapping and slang from his/her peers. Initiate discussions with your kids about drugs and the local drug scene, making the subject a shared area of interest. It is important for your child to recognize that you're interested in what is going on in his/her world.
>
> Keep the drug situation an open topic of conversation but do not depend on your children as your only source of information. Ask questions of other parents, teachers, youth counselors, narcotic officers and neighbors. Talk to your children's friends; they will often welcome the chance to open up with somebody other than their parents. Kids like to talk to adults—the more the better.
>
> *Make it clear that you will not allow your child to use drugs.* Take a firm intellectual and emotional stand and then spend a lot of time with your child. Do not argue with him/her when s/he is stoned on drugs or alcohol or when you are too angry to be coherent and reasonable. Talking with your child is the most important part of the process. This should not be a one-shot outburst or a ten-minute chat between appointments but

the beginning of an ongoing, open-ended discussion. Do not attack your child, put him/her down or sneer. S/he needs help!

A young person needs a reason not to smoke pot other than to be told "because I said so." The above article goes on to say:

> Let your child know why you are upset about his/her drug use. Tell your child what you have noticed about his/her behavior or moods or preoccupation. Tell your child why you are afraid of drug use. Don't become hysterical or exaggerate the dangers of drugs—you will only seem ridiculous and out of touch with reality. But don't be afraid to let your son or daughter know that you are hurt, disappointed and worried.

2. **Learn to "defuse" rebellion.** Marijuana was the protest drug of the sixties. It is no longer used by the masses of youth as an outward sign of rebellion, but it may be, on an individual basis. One youth told me, "I knew it would send my old man up a wall if he heard I was smoking pot. I wanted him to know—to hurt him."

His was a case of a broken father-son relationship. However, the lad was not only rebelling but crying out for attention. He wanted to be caught. More importantly, he wanted to be caught in his father's arms, or at least, gain some attention. It is sad but true that some kids can only be noticed by parents if they do something wrong or drastic to get attention.

I firmly believe parents can defuse rebellion, as I said in *Fast Track to Nowhere:*

> The time to watch is when children are between twelve and fourteen. Some do reach stages of rebellion sooner or even later, depending on circumstances at home and school. But generally speaking, the critical state and ages are twelve to fourteen. This is when the adolescent is trying to find himself and flex the emotional muscles of his very own individual personality. It is a period when he is full of contradictions, finding that he is torn between being the child of adolescence and becoming the emerging young adult.

Parents must remember that outside the home, kids are made to feel that to be "in" or to be accepted, they must drink or smoke a joint. Kids are torn between these two internal and external worlds at a time when it is normal for them to challenge their parents' standards and values and to see how far they can stretch the limits of parental authority. They are also trying to make up their minds as to their own personal convictions. Dr. Edward Bloomquist states in *Marijuana: The Second Trip:*

> There comes a time in a youngster's life when it is very important for him to isolate himself at times from his family to establish his own identity. Family activities up to the age of fourteen or fifteen are critical. At this point, however, parents should recognize that youngsters have a definite need to build their own particular world.

> Unfortunately, we are not always willing to let youth experiment. Yet when they become involved in activities which are abhorrent to parents, some adults may try to interrupt their "flight from the nest." This is an error because the child, if he is healthy, will find a way to escape even if it means alienating himself from his parents. Critically, youth needs support, emotional and frequently financial, from their parents up to and through their mid-twenties now that the educational jungle has extended its boundaries. Most cannot be cut off prematurely without serious psychological disruption, but neither will they permit adults to smother them if they have any aggressive spark of life.

In *Fast Track to Nowhere,* this is related to Christian youth:

> Christian youth, especially, go through periods of rebellion against the church and the things of God. They begin questioning the spiritual values and precepts they have been raised on. Such rebellion is natural and can produce positive results. Teens come to the age of "accountability" when they must choose for themselves as to whether they are going to follow Christ or Satan. Many choose to go their own way and only after years of wandering, does the prodigal come home.

Such rebellion does not need to lead to backsliding or kids getting "turned off" to the church and spiritual things. Parents can help by preparing for and accepting the fact of such rebellion. When the child is younger, the limits must be narrow. But the older the adolescent is, the wider must be the limit of his questioning and of permissible behavior. Ultimately, our youth have to make up their own minds about drugs, alcohol, sex, God, church, et cetera. As they mature, the limits need to be broadened until they are ready to make their own personal decisions.

3. **Listen for the "feel."** Words are windows to the soul. As was written in *Fast Track to Nowhere*, "Expressed rebellion can be a sign or signal to the parent of a deeper problem. Therefore, what the teenager is saying may not necessarily be what he means or 'feels.' *Listen for the feel."*

In the incident previously mentioned of the young man who said he wanted to hurt his father, he was in truth only reflecting his own internal hurt. It is a wise and discerning parent who is sensitive enough to know that behind his child's words and actions are feelings that may be a sign his child is saying something different or directly opposite from what appears on the surface.

The art of listening involves listening on three levels: listening to *what is said;* listening to *what has not been said* (what was left out); and listening for what *cannot* be said because it lies buried deep in the emotions.

Parents who have the right kind of relationship with a child will, on most occasions, know intuitively when the child is hurting or feeling down. Major doses of love and understanding will keep such a youngster from trying to block or escape the hurt by taking drugs and will encourage him to open up and talk about it.

4. **Let your teenager (or any child) know he or she is someone special.** Ann Landers, in an article printed in *Reader's Digest* entitled "What You Do and Don't Owe Your Children" states:

> What do parents owe their children? One of the chief obligations parents have to give their children is a sense of personal worth. Self-esteem is a cornerstone for good mental health. A

youngster who is continually criticized and "put down," made to feel stupid and inept, constantly compared with brothers, sisters, or cousins who do better, will become so unsure, so terrified of failing, that he or she won't try at all.

The child who is repeatedly called "bad" or "naughty" or "no good" will behave in a way that justifies the parents' description. Children have an uncanny way of living up—or down—to what is expected of them.

It is unfortunate that many parents were raised during the "silent years" when their parents never verbalized approval, only discipline. It has been carried over in this generation into two extremes: parents who give their children everything but praise, or parents who give their children neither.

5. **Establish firm and consistent rules.** Between parents and teens there are tensions—good ones—pulling at each other. One is the parents trying to enforce the limits they want their kids to operate within, and the kids stretching those or rewriting the line according to their own standards. In between the two lines, like tension wires, is what is popularly called "the generation gap." I believe such tensions are healthy. However, parents should stick to their standards, even though their kids are ultimately writing their own book of rules. Surprisingly, I find the troubled kids we work with want their parents to be strict (but fair). Even though they rebel and try to (and do) at times break the rules, deep down inside, they have a feeling that parents who bug them (in the right way) do care for them. Kids who grow up in families where the morals and standards are high and firm, yet applied with TLC (tender, loving care), grow up to be more mature, self-assured, and able to face the realities of life.

The recommendations made by *Focus on Alcohol and Drug Issues* state:

The number one and number two rules for today's parents should be: "Don't be afraid to be a strong parent" and "Don't be afraid of your children!"

In his book *Raising Children in a Difficult Time: A Philosophy of Parental Leadership and High Ideals* (1974), Dr. Spock emphasizes that parental timidity is the most common problem in child rearing in America today. He stresses that parents must function as grown-up mentors when raising teenagers, for parental uncertainty and inconsistency only confuse and anger adolescents.

Dr. Spock further urges parents not to lower their expectations on how adolescents should behave and, especially, not to worry that their strict standards will alienate their children or cause maladjustment. "Children are made comfortable in having been kept from wrongdoing or in paying for it. Underneath, they feel grateful to their parents. Naturally they won't thank you; they grumble or sulk temporarily, but this doesn't mean they have been disciplined unwisely. All children, being lawyers at heart, will experiment once or twice with trying to make parents feel guilty for some disapproval or punishment. If parents are unable to fend off such a reproach, children will surely bombard them with more."

Good home rule serves as an anchor and point of reference for kids as they get older. Families that establish standards that are rooted in Christian-Judaic teaching have the greater advantage and likelihood of success, in that it is a morality that can be reinforced when the children go away from home and have contact with a Christian community elsewhere. Parents whose home standards are "homemade" or are only vaguely religious usually lose control over their children once they are away from home.

As I explain to the young residents in our Christian rehabilitation program, "The program here is Jesus. Therefore when you graduate, the program will go with you everywhere you go." Parents who build their family life on the teachings and life of Jesus Christ are, in a sense, always united. They are linked by their common faith, common standards, and common truth.

6. **Be a "model" parent.** I believe one of the reasons for the rise in the number of kids turning to religious cults is because these organizations offer them group involvement, an authority figure, a caring community, and a sense of purpose and fulfillment—or, in a word, they are offered "a family." The Unification Church (the Moonies) in fact call themselves "the family."

Studies have shown that kids who drift into cult groups were prime candidates because there was something missing in their own family life. Dad and Mom were missing—not literally—but emotionally, physically and spiritually. Many of the cult kids had parents who were nonfunctioning. Business, a career, pursuing their own pleasures, and so forth, took them away from home, so they made up for it by giving their kids too much money and too much freedom and not enough of themselves.

Children and young people need models. They need flesh-and-blood models who take the time to flesh out Christianity and demonstrate to their kids that they practice what they preach.

Among cult groups, the teaching has very little to do with attracting kids. It is the fact that someone took the time to develop a one-to-one relationship with them, the fact that someone took them in. At Jonestown, nine hundred people died for their "father."

Parents, your kids are going to belong somewhere, or to something, and they are going to find someone to model—somewhere or anywhere—if they don't find one at home.

7. **Don't try to be perfect.** The number-one complaint of kids about parents is that they are hypocrites. It is dishonesty—not the failures of parents—that kids despise the most.

Parents who drink, use pills promiscuously, cheat or steal on a job, or are always trying to get around some law, then turn and pounce on their kids for something they did wrong, soon lose the child's respect. This cover-up, or need to try to be perfect in the eyes of the child, is not possible or necessary. Young people do not mind adults making mistakes as long as they are mature enough to acknowledge it when they make them. Anything less is hypocrisy and such parents have no right to expect their kids to be any different from themselves. Many parents whose kids give them trouble are merely reaping the seeds the parents themselves have sown by their misdeeds.

Some other parents, especially religious ones, develop a very rigid life-style, in which they always try to live by the letter of the law. This is to be commended but such rigidity can turn into legalism and result in a home where the parents are hard but not happy, tough but not tender, firm without feeling, and living under law without grace.

It is impossible to live perfect lives, and our children know it. The sooner parents show it, the more credibility and respect they will have from their kids.

8. **A family that "is together" has a better opportunity of staying together.** One of the kindest comments one teenager can make to another is, "Boy, your family is really together." They are, of course, not just referring to physical togetherness but to the emotional, philosophical, and spiritual unity that is a rarity nowadays.

I believe in the slogan "a family that prays together stays together." This points out, however, only one aspect of wholesome family life—the spiritual side. There is another side—the social side. An imbalance in either direction does more harm than good.

I can hear a mother or father saying, "All that sounds good, but my kid is beyond prevention. He is already smoking pot. What can I do?" The following is a list of simple but important recommended steps for parents who discover their teenager is using drugs. While the list is far from exhaustive, these at least are attempts to do the right thing in the right way.

Is Your Teenager Using Drugs?

1. **Know the signs that help to tell if your child is on drugs.** Asking, "Can I know if my child is using drugs?" is not unlike asking if you can tell if your child is awake or asleep. I am quite positive about this matter. Parents who are close to their kids, spend quality time with them, and have good personal relationships with them will know when something is wrong. When you really care about somebody, you know when something is bothering them.

Some of the early warning signals of a developing problem are:

Mood changes—a pleasant child may turn cynical, pessimistic, or moody
Lowered energy level—may become restless, sleeping longer or at odd times, nervous, changing from aggressive to passive, apathetic
Undependability—a normally helpful, attentive child may become forgetful, vague, and seem to be out of it
Loss of self-confidence—the child may even feel op-

pressed—"somebody is out to get me"—having feelings of being persecuted or oppressed

WARNING! These signs, in and of themselves, are not absolute evidence that your child is using drugs. They could symbolize a physical or emotional problem brought on by something else. But these *are* signs that something is wrong, and it is the duty of a parent to find out if that something could be drug abuse.

There are also other signs parents can pick up such as: *evading responsibility; attendance at school affected; disappearing at unusual times and for unusual lengths of time and with some unusual explanation; change in clothing style; a new and suspicious circle of friends; unusual odor in the teenager's room; the buying and burning of candles, and so forth.*

2. **Don't overreact.** Hearing your child is on dope may sound much worse than it is. In spite of fifteen years of greater public awareness of the drug problem, many parents do not really understand the difference between drug use, drug abuse, and drug addiction. To say that someone is "on drugs" or "using dope" may mean experimentation, or it could be regular use. And smoking pot is different from popping a pill and certainly vastly different from sniffing coke (cocaine) or injecting heroin into the vein.

"I feel the thing to do is to sit down and go through the old 'what, who, why, when, and where' type of thinking," states Dr. Edward R. Bloomquist in a pamphlet entitled *The Real Dope on Pot.* He continues, "The most important thing is for adults carefully, and I emphasize carefully, to take stock of the situation."

I believe there is a very short, yet vitally important, period when a youngster begins experimenting with drugs, when the parent has the best opportunity to nip it in the bud. After this period (however long it may last) when the teenager gets deeper into drugs and the drug culture, it becomes increasingly difficult to get him/her to stop.

During this first discovery of drug use, avoid undue criticism, chastisement, or becoming so emotionally distraught that things are said in the heat of anger which are later regretted, because this can widen the gap between parent and teenager. This may drive his drug use underground or even push him deeper into it. Let parents panic inside—not outside. In the privacy of the bedroom or when seeking counsel of a minister or trusted friend, is a time to let distress out. But when trying to get to the bottom of a child's drug taking, calmness and sanity with firmness are important. Dr. Bloomquist points out one other important result of a kid's drug use that can cause parents to lose their perspective in the matter and prevent proper reaction on their part. He states:

> Parents usually ask, "Where did I go wrong?" This is really not as pertinent as many people think. The "parent blamers" overlook the fact that in the majority of instances, the parent couldn't have prevented his child from taking drugs. Today's youth are mobile, they readily intercommunicate, and most have a financial background that permits them to acquire and do almost anything they want.

A publication released by the National Institute on Drug Abuse, entitled *Prevention Resources,* talked about a group of parents in Georgia who decided to take a stand against what they considered a cultural rift in their community that resulted in many of their children abusing marijuana. The pamphlet stated:

> ... first shocked and disbelieving, the parents began facing the facts at home and began looking beyond the family to see what was happening to their children. After going through the "guilt bag" they decided that if all their caring concern for their children, the comfortable, too-affluent life-styles, their education and professional backgrounds and values did not qualify them to assert themselves against a seeming consensus that marijuana is okay, they had better find out if their alarm was justified.... Instead of shaking their heads about the way things seemed, they began preparing to make changes....

3. **Don't ignore drug use.** According to one report, only three out of ten teenagers believe that their parents know about their pot smoking. According to one seventeen-year-old who was quoted in the book *The Private Life of the American Teenager:*

> Half the time parents have no idea because kids are pretty good at keeping things hidden. If you sleep over at a friend's house and get bombed or stoned, you don't go home till

you're sober. Your parents go around happy in their illusions that everything is okay. What a joke! Parents are really dumb if they think kids aren't doing things just because they've never actually caught them in the act.

If and when some parents do discover their children's drug involvement, they may not be able to stop it but for sure, they must not ignore it. Occasional pot smoking by some young people can quickly turn into regular, habitual smoking or—worse—to the use of hard drugs.

One mother said, "I was not only shocked to find my daughter was smoking pot, but she was doing it on a regular basis. Either she was very careful to hide the signs from me or I was very naïve."

If kids are discreet, as the above quoted teenager stated, they can keep parents from knowing they're on pot for a long time. Some are even deceptive—living one life at home or church and another at school or with friends. However, once it is discovered, it is time to take action.

Taking action does not necessarily mean parents can get their children to stop smoking pot, although that is or should be the goal. The best parents can hope for is abstinence; the least is establishing a line of communication to help if the drug taking gets too far out of hand. Maggie, the daughter of Susan Bromwell, quoted in the article "How I Got My Daughter to Stop Smoking Pot," told her mother:

> Mom, except for one thing, you handled my pot problem just right. Parents should show their concern and should give their kids medical findings about pot. The thing you did wrong was let me smoke in the house. You should have said, "I'm letting you make the decision as to whether you're going to smoke pot or not. But part of that decision is accepting the consequences—not only of the possibility of getting busted but of what pot can do to you." If kids have access to pot and they think it's harmless—as most kids do—they're definitely going to get to abuse it. . . .

Of course, if it's younger kids who are doing the smoking, parents should insist they do not smoke, inside or outside the home, or disciplinary measures will be taken.

4. **Learn everything you can about the dangers of drugs.** The parents' group mentioned previously, called the DeKalb (Georgia) Families in Action, Inc. (DFIA), decided, "Instead of shaking their heads about the way things seem, they began preparing to make changes."

Among other positive actions, they gathered a wide range of literature, going both to the head shops, to see what their kids were reading, and to the library for the latest medical evidence. After their research, "They became more rather than less concerned about the effects of marijuana. They discovered that the information about marijuana most likely to fall into the hands of young people minimizes the dangers of marijuana as contrasted with alcohol...."

"The evidence they found was ample to assure them that marijuana was no innocuous weed or a sophisticated pacifier for children on the brink of, or in the midst of, their second most important developmental year, puberty."

5. **Try to mentally "detoxify" the drug user.** I use this term *detoxify* not in a physical sense, for marijuana does *not* physically addict anyone, but in a psychological sense. The parents, after careful reading and research on marijuana (as the DeKalb County, Georgia, group did) should take the right opportunity to mentally and psychologically detoxify their child's thinking about marijuana. I am convinced that, with the right information given in the right way to youth, many will make the right decision about smoking pot. However this must be done early, preferably before the youngster has even experimented.

6. **Join or organize parent-action groups to fight drug abuse in the schools and community.** Sadly, most schools, parent groups, and other civic organizations let down on their drug awareness after the LSD, heroin, and pill epidemic of the sixties and early seventies. During the past five to eight years, in the meantime, the decriminalization laws have gone into effect, and a nationwide discussion of possible legalization has created a whole new pot-smoking populace. Parents have done little to counteract this.

Hats off to the DeKalb, Georgia, parents, who felt the issue on drug abuse deeply enough:

... to organize a campaign against apathy, ignorance, denial, and confusion in their neighborhood. After the parents began to check out the paraphernalia shops that had mushroomed in the metropolitan and suburban areas ... questions led to actions, headlines, and before long, changes in the laws of Georgia governing the sale of drug-related objects to minors ... the organization can now take credit for making a sizeable impact on the consciousness of more than one state about the desirability of coming to terms with marijuana as a concomitant of adolescence.

If marijuana is decriminalized or legalized, it will only be because the lawmakers are responding to the voice or silence of the voters and the public at large.

Marsha Keith Schuchard, a founding member of the DeKalb Families in Action, has set forth some steps for concerned parents to follow in getting to the bottom of a local drug-related problem. Here is the list of her suggestions:

Organize a group of committed and concerned parents who want to find out if there is a problem in the local schools and community—and to what extent.

Do something with the information you find. Don't just blame the kids, the school, or look for scapegoats. Be ready to confront the parents of known users and suppliers with a motive to help, not hurt.

Work with local agencies that are credible and able to help.

Tell the kids at home what you are doing and why.

Take a clear and firm stand *against any drug usage by your child*.... Whatever your rule, make it clear and consistent.

Get all parents committed to enforcing prevention rules—and to punish violators.

Encourage frequent and lengthy home discussions between parents and kids.

Provide alternative activities for youth in the community.

Recognize that it will not be all sweetness and light. Kids who are cocooned into a drug-using peer group will fight to maintain that secure circle of friends. They can be sullen, defiant, deceptive, and downright dislikeable. A parent has to hang in there, to act out of pure faith, for a long time to make his or her child recognize her seriousness. This may take a few months or a few years. But, a parent owes it to the child. The alternatives are too hazardous. A child's drug usage can tear a family apart, but a parental and family struggle to regain a drug-free child can strengthen and reunify a family.

Provide for some ongoing parent communication network to deal with any other problems that may arise among youth. It is easier to prevent than correct.

The above material and direct quotes were taken from Dr. Schuchard's speech to the South East Drug Conference, May 25, 1978, and published in the National Institute on Drug Abuse's *Prevention Resources,* Winter 1978. Address: 5600 Fishers Lane, Room 10-A-56, Rockville, MD 20857. The address of DeKalb Families in Action is 1436 Cornell Rd., NE, Atlanta, GA 30303.

7. **Let your feelings be known to your state legislators.** If or when a bill comes up before your state legislators, send a letter to your local representative and let your concerns be known. If marijuana becomes legalized, we have no one to blame but ourselves.

9
The Courage to Say No!

In the game of football, there is an expression "A good offense is the best defense." The team that keeps control of the ball offensively usually does not have to have its defensive team on the field a lot. This keeps the defense fresh and strong and better able to stop the other team's offense. In other words, control the football and you control the game. The chances of winning are better then. The best "game plan" in life is to know how to control one's own body, mind, and soul—and thus control one's destiny. If not, other people and forces will gain control. Those who abuse their bodies and minds with drugs often have no offense in life. They have no goals, no purpose in life, little motivation, and no defense against the pressure from peers or other seductive forces within society. The J. B. Phillips translation of the apostle Paul's writing to the Romans reads: ". . . Don't let the world around you squeeze you into its own mould . . ." (12:2).

Resisting Drugs

How can the "squeezers" be resisted? How can young people find the courage and power to say *no* to drugs? There is what psychologists label a "herd" instinct in society, which young people especially fall prey to. This is the pressure to conform, to be and do what everyone else is doing. Everyone seems cut out of the same cookie cutter. Many find security in sameness. We are a nation of imitators. Many strive to be so different from their parents and the older generation, yet among peers, the pressure to conform is so powerful as to squeeze every ounce of individuality out of the younger generation. It is therefore a great challenge to help young people find both inner and outer resources to walk to the beat of a different drummer. How rare, but how refreshing, to find a young man or young lady today who has heeded the words of Solomon from Proverbs 1:10: "My son, if sinners entice thee, consent thou not."

It is possible to withstand the enticers and to keep from falling prey to all the destructive fads and fancies of a youth culture. I have seen the evidence in the lives of those who found the courage to say no and not experiment with pot in the first place. And I've seen those who did fall into the drug trap overcome their habit and addiction, and become clean and stay clean. In my work with addicted and troubled youth, I have seen literally thousands healed and rehabilitated from the horrors of hard-core narcotic addiction and drug abuse. I never cease to be amazed at their testimonies. The grace and power of God in transforming these social lepers is a modern-day miracle.

But equally exciting is to witness the faith and faithfulness of young people who never fall into the trap in the first place and who "walk not in the counsel of the ungodly, nor stand in the way of sinners, nor sit in the seat of the scornful" (*see* Psalms 1:1), the scornful being those who laughed and said, "Come on, what's wrong with smoking a joint?"

What does it take to keep pure and clean? Can our children and youth find the intestinal fortitude and the willpower to say no to drugs? In spite of the fact that 40 to 50 million Americans have experimented with marijuana (the majority being under 25 years of age), it is also a fact that at least 30 percent or more of our youth do not smoke pot. True, the number of "tokers" is growing daily. However, millions have never experimented, and many who have, did not choose to make it a regular part of their life-style. Why didn't they? What causes some kids to go straight and others to smoke?

How to Say *No*

The following are a few helpful hints for young people wanting to find the courage to say no, so they "Don't copy the behavior and customs of this world, but be a new and different person with a fresh newness in all you do and think . . ." (Romans 12:2 TLB). Because these suggestions are based on the teachings of the Bible, they are best understood and experienced and obtainable by those who have a personal relationship with Jesus Christ. However, the Bible contains good advice for every young person who is willing to listen. I have seen youth influenced by the teaching of the Bible, even though they did not accept Christ into their lives. Of course good

The Courage to Say No!

advice or good living will not help people get into heaven, but it may help them get along better on earth until they commit their lives fully to Jesus Christ. Here are some helpful hints in finding the courage to say no:

1. **Respect your body.** "I beseech you therefore, brethren, by the mercies of God, that ye present your bodies a living sacrifice, holy, acceptable unto God, which is your reasonable service" (Romans 12:1).

"What? know ye not that your body is the temple of the Holy Ghost which is in you, which ye have of God, and ye are not your own?" (1 Corinthians 6:19).

Those who are God-fearing acknowledge there is a Supreme ownership of their bodies. The Bible teaches that we are His (God's) "offspring"—"fearfully and wonderfully made." When we abuse the body we abuse His body. Nowhere does it state in the Bible that we should not smoke cigarettes or pot. Yet many Christians believe it is wrong to smoke either, and, like myself, do not indulge in the drinking of alcoholic beverages. Where does this conviction come from? From the teaching contained in the above-quoted verses and others that are similar. We are to present acceptable bodies unto God. We are to live in our bodies as we act in a temple (church). We are to respect our bodies as we respect a temple—a holy place.

The argument some pot smokers use to justify their right to pollute their bodies is that they feel that "it is my body. I can do with it whatever I please."

God says that it is not so. But even apart from this Christian teaching, I believe society has a right to expect the government to institute laws to protect youth from themselves—not to allow them to abuse their bodies. The right to use drugs violates the rights of others when we examine the effects marijuana has on automobile drivers, on the male sperm and the female reproductive organs (someone must protect the innocent children that could be born defective from a pot-smoking parent). I have a right to be assured that my auto mechanic, airplane-maintenance workers, and others responsible for delivering essential services are not stoned with pot when they are on the job.

I could make a long list of people who could violate my rights by being under the influence of marijuana on the job or when in daily contact with other people (my kids' schoolteacher, bus driver, subway conductor, nurse, physician, lifeguard, fireman, and so forth). Just as I am entitled to sit in a nonsmoking section of an airplane or restaurant so I don't get cancer fumes blown in my face, so I am entitled not to have my human and social rights violated—either directly or indirectly—as the result of another person's altered perceptions, thinking, reasoning, or reactions while under the influence of marijuana. Another person's right ends where my safety and well-being begins, and it begins as soon as I step out of the door of my house.

If someone wants to smoke pot in the privacy of his own home or in some remote mountain cabin and inhale till his brain is saturated with the stuff, I have no right to deny him that privilege. But as soon as he steps into public territory and goes on the streets, or heads out onto the highway where I am driving, or reports to a job where I might have to go for his services, or enters a classroom with my son or daughter, or comes in contact with the human race in any way, shape, or form, he is responsible for respecting my rights, my lungs, my safety, my body, and my life.

I'm already paying a higher rate of taxes and insurance (auto and health) because of increased deaths, injury, and disease on the part of cigarette smokers and alcohol abusers; I don't want to have to pay an even higher rate as a result of the damage done in our society by the legislation of marijuana.

Apparently neither did a Long Island railroad employee. A conductor on the Long Island Railroad had to leave his train because of a headache and nausea he got from what he termed the "pot train." His car of the train was filled with young people headed for a rock concert.

"I don't know whether it was marijuana, hashish, or something else," he said, "but the smoke was so thick you could hardly see one end of the car from the other," he stated, in an article entitled "LIRR 'Pot Train' Ticket Taker Is Feeling Punchy," which appeared in the *New York Post*.

He reported the situation to his supervisor and was told he should sign out sick, but he wouldn't do it, because he would lose three days' sick pay.

Both the laws of God and the laws of man teach us to have a healthy respect for our own bodies, as well as those of others.

2. Keep your eyes on the goalposts. A young football player became a born-again Christian. He was asked how he expected to keep from getting down or defeated in an atmosphere of cursing, dirty jokes, drinking, and carousing. The idea was also suggested to him that it might be best if he quit playing the game. He answered, "I know it's not going to be easy to live a Christian life—but I've already learned to keep my eyes on the goalposts and not look at the spiritual opposition when I come to the scrimmage line of life. I look beyond the evil around me, to see Jesus. The Bible says, 'Where your treasure is there will your heart be also.' "

He had learned that one of the secrets to success in life as a Christian is to set his affections on things above and not on the earth. Many youth are like the fellow who threw a dart on the wall, then went over and drew a circle around it. They aim at anything, and hit it every time. They do not live for tomorrow. They have set no goalposts before them. They don't know who they are, why they are, or where they are going.

For these drifters, smoking pot makes sense; they have nothing else to shoot for. They have no commitment to life, to a moral philosophy, religion, God, or even themselves. They are on a fast track to nowhere. Solomon, in Proverbs 1:31, describes what happens to the youth who has no goal and thus does whatever he wants: "That is why you must eat the bitter fruit of having your own way, and experience the full terrors of the pathway you have chosen" (TLB).

The sad plight of the lost youth I observe is not just what they are, but what they are not. They sit on the sideline (or bleachers) of life and never get in the game. Talents are wasted, education dropped, energy drained, bodies abused, minds polluted. The waste of human potential among the physically and intellectually young is an appalling waste of our gross-national human product. I have witnessed the tragedy of young men whose bodies have become that of an older man, their emotions so stunted they never developed beyond adolescence, and with an education of a child, plus the wisdom of a fool. *Future* is not in their vocabulary. Their past is only a record in the courts. I weep for them. The media refer to some of them as the "throw-away generation." Either they have been thrown out by parents and society or they have chosen to throw away their lives themselves.

Thank God there is another silent but potent minority who have found through their faith in God that there is a "game plan" to life. They look to Christ and the Word of God to give them the goalpost to aim for. They learn, for example, from Proverbs 4:23–27:

> Keep thy heart with all diligence; for out of it are the issues of life. Put away from thee a froward mouth, and perverse lips put far from thee [this includes putting a joint to the lips]. Let thine eyes look right on, and let thine eyelids look straight before thee. Ponder the path of thy feet, and let all thy ways be established. Turn not to the right hand nor to the left: remove thy foot from evil.

At the age of twelve, I knew what I wanted to be at the age of sixteen. At sixteen I knew where and what I wanted to be at eighteen. And at eighteen I knew what I wanted to do with my life at twenty-five. Since adolescence, I can never remember not having goalposts before me. Many was the occasion when the lure of the crowd and the temptation of the present loomed large before my eyes. But far ahead, as the above proverb so simply states, I "let my eyelids look straight before me," and there were the goalposts. It made it easier to choose between present folly and future reward.

3. **Guard relationships.** Former pot smokers tell me the main thing that influenced them to experiment with drugs was pressure from friends. Peer pressure seems to be stronger today than with previous generations. The mass media also contribute to the philosophy of "everyone's doin' it." Movies, television, radio, and the music industry scream out to kids and influence their thinking and life-style. Parents very quickly become, in many cases, the secondary influence over their children's thinking and decision making. Whether it be the lyrics of the latest hit tune or the slogan on a T-shirt, the message is the same: Turn on with sex, drugs, booze.

It is not drugs that kids want or fear the most: it's losing face among peers that is a fate worse than anything. To be "uncool" will cause a young person to make certain radical choices. If smoking pot or drinking is the initiation fee they have to pay to be accepted and respected by the street culture, they'll willingly pay the price. If "getting it on" gets them "in," then they are willing, ready, and able to participate.

"Kids turn on kids," said one young man, "not drugs, drink, or pushers." Therefore, it's not what kids have in common that brings them together; it's what they *do* in common. Relationships are often very shallow and superficial. It's not personalities coming together—it's bodies. It's not being together that counts; it's *doing* together.

It all gets boring quickly. Conversation has to be spiced with drugs or drink. Sex has to be boosted with a high. And the next time around, the joint may have to be more potent, the drug a little more powerful.

Youth who want to avoid drug abuse must avoid certain persons; they must guard their relationships. Friends must be chosen not only on the basis of who the person is, but who he hangs around with. I told one young lady, who was about to begin a relationship with a certain young man, "Remember, when you accept Charlie, you're going to have to accept his friends. He may be okay on a one-to-one relationship with you, but you may also be buying a ticket into a crowd whose habits are not what you bargained for when you started dating Charlie."

A wrong relationship can lead to a wrong environment, which in turn can lead to a wrong decision. Anyone who wants to guard his behavior must first guard his relationships.

When choosing friends, it is wise to heed the instructions contained in Proverbs 2:11–15 (NIV):

> Discretion will protect you,
>   and understanding will guard you.
> Wisdom will save you from the ways of wicked men,
>   from men whose words are perverse,
> who leave the straight paths
>   to walk in dark ways,
> who delight in doing wrong
>   and rejoice in the perverseness of evil,
> whose paths are crooked
>   and who are devious in their ways.

4. **A reason to say "No."** I understand why kids turn to pot. Something has to make them feel good. If the mind is not clean, if the body is not under subject of the spirit and soul of the person, if the heart is empty—artificial stimulants and mind-altering sub-

stances become necessary evils to provide temporary happiness and peace of mind. Now not all marijuana smokers are social dropouts or uncommitted individuals. Some smoke to escape the pressure of school, work or just ordinary daily living. The fact that they have not found satisfaction from within themselves makes it necessary for them to go to some other source.

To be born again is to live life on a spiritual plane. Jesus promised believers that when He dwelt within them, "out of your inner most being shall flow rivers of living water." Jesus also stated: "But whosoever drinketh of the water that I shall give him shall never thirst; but the water that I shall give him shall be in him a well of water springing up into everlasting life" (John 4:14). Some things add life, but Christ is life. Christians are motivated by a perpetual source of life—an eternal flame, to use another analogy—that need not be bought. They have a reason to say no. To the unbeliever, it is difficult to understand that Christians have a reason to avoid evil habits. A man who can eat steak will not eat dog food. A man who has experienced the supernatural high does not need the unnatural high.

"Those who let themselves be controlled by their lower natures live only to please themselves, but those who follow after the Holy Spirit find themselves doing those things that please God." Why? Because "Following after the Holy Spirit leads to life and peace [without drugs], but following after the old nature leads to death, because the old sinful nature within us is against God . . ." (Romans 8:5–7 TLB).

In lower-nature living, it is as normal to smoke pot as it is for the spiritually minded to want to worship God. Christians do not keep away from sin and evil just because they are afraid of breaking commandments, although this is a part of the motivation. There is a higher reason for saying no. That reason is rooted in the love relationship with Jesus Christ. I love to hear former drug addicts sing these words by John Peterson: "I thirsted in the barren land of sin and shame, and nothing satisfying there I found, then one day to the cross of Jesus Christ I came, where thirsting spirits can be satisfied."

Those who have a reason to say no are the satisfied customers. They have tasted and seen that the Lord is good. "It's the greatest high I've ever experienced," said one former drug abuser. I realize some may resent the use of the word *high* to describe the Christian experience, but we must remember that the new convert still relates his newfound joy to the vocabulary and life-style of his past. In this light, we should be able to appreciate that he is trying to say that Jesus Christ is so much greater and better than anything he experienced in the drug culture.

5. **"No" Power!** A young Christian convert, with a past history of drug abuse, returned from his first visit to the old neighborhood since his new way of life. A broad smile crossed his face as he said, "I came face-to-face with my old friends. They didn't believe I had changed. They offered me my choice of pot, pills, booze or coke [cocaine]—all free. I said no thanks. As I got ready to leave them one hollered out, 'You'll be back—I bet.'

"I don't intend to. I said no for the first time in my life. It feels good to be free. Now I know it's true what I've read in the Bible—whom the son [Jesus Christ] sets free, is free indeed."

This is the *no power;* that is, the power to refuse evil and do good, that I speak of. Many youth have all the reasons in the world, and in the world to come, to say no, yet they still give in to fleshly indulgences. Why? They lack the power to say no.

One of the main reasons youth—especially street kids—give for not accepting Christ is the fear of failure and phoniness. Many are so geared to failure they don't understand there is a power available to them to be successful in the Christian way of life.

"This is the tremendous thing about coming to Christ," I explain to those hungry to receive the power to say no. "He doesn't call us to Himself without giving us what we need to be the Christian the Bible tells us we should be. He knows your past, your problems, your hang-ups, your record, your handicaps—He doesn't want you to fall or fail any more than you do. This is why the Bible says, '... as many as received him, to them gave he power to become the sons of God ...'" (John 1:12).

Yes, power to *become.* The receiver becomes, among other things, a soldier instead of a slave. He attacks life, rather than retreating from it. He says *no* instead of *yes* to evil and wrong.

Examples of this *no* power or power to say no abound both in biblical history and all around us today.

Think of Moses. He refused to become the Pharaoh's yes-man. "It was by faith that Moses, when he grew up, refused to be treated as the grandson of the king, but chose to share ill-treatment with God's people instead of enjoying the fleeting pleasures of sin" (Hebrews 11:24, 25 TLB). The key word is *refused*.

What about the handsome, well-dressed, robust young man named Joseph?

> One day at about this time Potiphar's wife began making eyes at Joseph, and suggested that he come and sleep with her.
>
> Joseph refused. "Look," he told her, "my master trusts me with everything in the entire household; he himself has no more authority here than I have! He has held back nothing from me except you yourself because you are his wife. How can I do such a wicked thing as this? It would be a great sin against God."
>
> But she kept on with her suggestions day after day, even though he refused to listen, and kept out of her way as much as possible.
>
> Genesis 39:7–10 TLB

No! No! No! Joseph made it loud and clear. So can the Joes of today.

A *yes* to Christ is a *no* to the evil environment out of which comes pot and other harmful habits.

The unsung heroes of our day—the superstars in the eyes of the Lord—are those who have said no to drugs and instead have said, "I'd rather have Jesus."